PRAISE FOR *PREGNANT FATHERS*—

"Jack Heinowitz has helped thousands of fathers—and mothers—over the years approach parenting as a shared journey and adventure. *Pregnant Fathers* should be required reading for every man who has the honor and privilege of setting out on that adventure."

Richard Louv
Author of *Childhood's Future, FatherLove,*
and *101 Things You Can Do for Our Children*

"'Pregnant' men . . . need much the same nurturance and education as pregnant women. This little gem of a book offers needed guidelines to point the way. May we follow them!"

Robbie E. Davis-Floyd, PhD
Author of *Birth As an American Rite of Passage*

"Jack Heinowitz confronts the reality of new fatherhood. In the process, he helps men realize how important they are as husbands and fathers. A much needed recognition and encouragement."

Tine Thevenin
Author of *The Family Bed: An Age-Old Concept in Childrearing* and *Mothering and Fathering: The Gender Differences in Childrearing*

"An engaging, authoritative guidebook to the pregnancy experience from the husband's point of view."

Sam Osherson, PhD
Author of *Finding Our Fathers* and *Wrestling with Love*

"One of those books that make one say, 'Now why didn't someone do this long ago?'"

Eda LeShan
Author of *When Your Child Drives You Crazy*

"This book is a *must!!!*"

Stan Dale, DHS
Author of *My Child, My Self: How to Raise the Child You Always Wanted to Be*

"This book answers the major questions men often want to ask but are shy to express."

Gayle Peterson, PhD
Author of *An Easier Childbirth* and *Birthing Normally*

PREGNANT FATHERS

Entering Parenthood Together

PREGNANT FATHERS

Entering Parenthood Together

Jack Heinowitz, PhD

Foreword by David B. Chamberlain, PhD

Parents As Partners Press
San Diego, California

Published by: **Parents As Partners Press**
4026 Hawk Street, Suite H
San Diego, CA 92103

Front cover photo by Dave Rusk
Back cover photo by Hugh Stone
Cover art by Carol Landry
Cover design and graphics by DynaPac/Lee Aellig and Artmania
Edited by Ellen Kleiner
Book design by Richard Harris
Illustration by Betsy James
Illustration typography by John Inserra

Library of Congress Cataloging-in-Publication Data
Heinowitz, Jack.
    Pregnant fathers.
    Bibliography: pp.
    Index.
    1. Pregnancy. 2. Pregnancy—Psychological aspects.
3. Childbirth. 4. Fathers. 5. Parenting. I. Title.
RG525.H42   618.2   AACR2
1995

ISBN 0-9641024-0-4
Manufactured in the United States of America
Library of Congress Catalog Card Number: 95-66608
            10 9 8 7 6 5 4 3 2 1

PHOTO CREDITS—Suzanne Arms: pages x, 22, 23, 25, 39, 40, 51, 68, 91, 128, 135, 149, 156, 170. Anna Propp Covici: pages 67, 78. Ellen Eichler: pages 4, 76, 174. Jill Fineberg: page 41. Jan Francisco: page 151. Jack Heinowitz: page 132. Rose Jurman: page 182. Mary Motley Kalergis: pages 55, 94, 119, 122, 125, 140, 162. Marilyn Nolt: page 165. Leah Olman: page 155. Miguel Pisarro: pages 86, 103. Teri Preston: page 123. Dave Rusk: page 81. Michael Weisbrot: pages 18, 38, 43, 71, 158, 178, 188.

In Gratitude

My HEARTFELT THANKS to all those who encouraged and supported me in doing this one my way. It has been a labor of love and a bountiful birth!

To Joyce, for your interest and generosity; Dena, for your optimism and contagiously high energy; Anne, for your enthusiasm and expertise; Beth, for your calm confidence and steady know-how; Pam, for your reassurance and camaraderie; Steve, for your friendship and assorted clippings; Ian, for your levity and reliable follow-through; and Debby, for reminding me that the message and the dream are just as important now as they were then. And to Ron and Sylvia, for bringing us into the fold at this auspicious time—your trust helped me let down and reexperience the joyfulness of new birth.

To my mentors: Paul Brenner, for leading me into new dimensions of creativity; Erving and Miriam Polster, Cathy Conheim, and Leie Carmody, for sharing and guiding my unfolding.

To the men I interviewed, for their openness and courage. And to my clients, for their determination to push through fear and pain, to heal, and to become participants in life, and for keeping me honest.

To Dad, for showing me that acceptance, warmth, feeling, and doing are all at the heart of father love.

To Mom, for instilling your dedication and reliability; for your sustenance and caring, always.

To Eden, for embracing me as dad and helping stretch my love in new directions, and for your kind forgiveness and resilience.

To Becky (Cole), for returning—to my great delight—to dance and play again, and for sharing your poetic ways and your passion for each moment. Such gifts you bring, lovely daughter.

To Jesse, for rearranging my life so magnificently, for awakening my little boy, and for evoking such wonderful childhood memories. You bring me more love, vitality, and purpose than I ever imagined. And so much more to come. Lead the way.

To Ellen, cherished partner and easy friend, for believing in me from the start; for beaming encouragement and gentleness; for joining me in our midlife journeying; for the late-night lullabies for three; and for caring for the family so I could step to my own rhythm.

To Ellen, young love, dear new friend. How strange and wonderful to join up again. Gatherer of lists, effervescent cheerleader, deep editor par excellence, most trustworthy and able midwife in this unexpected and wonderful birthing. You're invaluable and dearly appreciated.

Contents

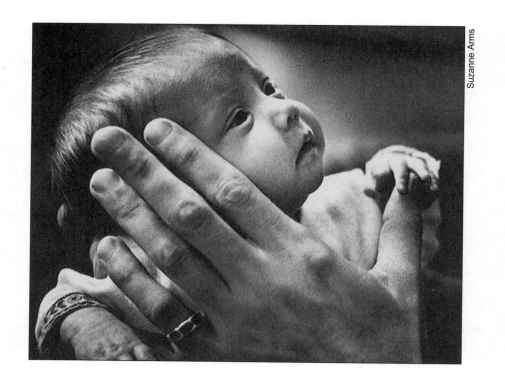

I'll walk in the rain by your side. I'll cling to the warmth of your tiny hand. I'll do anything to help you understand. I'll love you more than anybody can.

—John Denver
"For Baby"

FATHERS ARE PREGNANT TOO! Few people acknowledge this marvelous fact of life. Few books mention it. This guidebook to fatherhood spells it all out.

Becoming a father is a life-changing adventure, and not necessarily an easy one. Fatherhood raises all sorts of questions taking you back to childhood and the quality of your experiences with *your* father. If your relationship with your father was good, you will be propelled through pregnancy by rich memories and eager anticipation. If your relationship was unsatisfactory, then you have some work to do. Pregnancy can be your wake-up call to resolve old issues and *choose* the type of father you want to be to your child.

Fortunately, the journey from conception to birth takes time— exactly what is needed to awaken deep-down feelings and learn to share needs, anxieties, and hopes. Fortunately, too, babies start working their magic before they are born. The growing baby in the womb pushes things steadily forward, transforming a woman into a mother, a man into a father, and a couple into a family.

During the 266 incredible days of pregnancy, the mystical connections between family members become tangible: the baby depends on the mother who depends on the father who depends on the love of wife and baby. Life becomes circular, continuous, and transforming. *Fatherhood is enlarging.*

Fathers are desperately needed. Too often, however, men do not realize how needed they are. Sweeping through our cities and towns is a crippling plague: the "vanishing father" epidemic. Each year, 30 percent of all babies in the United States are born fatherless. In some large cities, as many as 50 to 70 percent are born to a

1

father who has disappeared! Many of the mothers left behind give birth prematurely to low-birthweight babies who begin languishing in the womb. Their future is no brighter, for they are subject to a higher than average rate of mortality in infancy and a strong likelihood of physical, emotional, social, and economic problems throughout life.

Fathers make a huge difference to mothers and babies not only during pregnancy, but at birth. Any man who has been there is forever touched and changed. He bonds in a profound way to his partner and to the new human being their lovemaking has brought to them. The presence of a willing and comfortable father at birth also diminishes the mother's perception of pain, decreases her use of drugs, increases her stamina, and helps her reveal her true maternal power—perhaps for the first time.

In whatever environment you choose for the big event, be prepared to slip into your own fatherly trance, absorbed in the rhythms of the laboring mother and ready to be a sustaining, supportive presence. This will be a new kind of labor for you both. Your purpose is to be there for her; her purpose is to do the real work of bringing the baby down through the birth canal and out for that first incredible face-to-face meeting.

No one is ever fully prepared for the riveting encounter with an infant's penetrating, knowing eyes. After an awed silence, you may begin talking to your newborn, feeling a little foolish for thinking that this person can understand what you are saying. No matter, talk on. The latest scientific studies indicate that babies are much smarter than we ever imagined. Bypassing language and reading your mind directly, your baby may *very well* get the gist of your message. At the very least, having heard your voice all these months yet having no idea what you look like, your baby will search your face with immense curiosity.

Seeing you at last, your baby may imitate your facial expressions. Displays of happiness, sadness, or surprise flow easily from parent to child. Stick out your tongue, open your mouth wide, and your baby may follow suit. If the birth experience was especially good, your baby may even reward you with a smile!

Fatherhood beckons. Pregnancy is for answering the call. This book will show you the way.

Heart to heart and man to man, Jack Heinowitz takes you safely through thrilling and scary territory. Escorting you on the fatherly journey from conception through the first year of parenthood, he offers psychologically sound counsel inspired by his own experience and sprinkled with the collective wisdom gathered by other men traversing the challenging path to fatherhood. Free of dogma and demands, this user-friendly guidebook will give you plenty of room to feel what *you* feel and lots of practical options for working things out with your partner along the way.

With book in hand, take heart and move toward fully engaged fathering!

DAVID B. CHAMBERLAIN, PHD
PRESIDENT OF THE ASSOCIATION FOR
PRE- AND PERINATAL PSYCHOLOGY AND HEALTH

THE FIRST EDITION OF *PREGNANT FATHERS* was born out of my graduate dissertation entitled "Becoming a Father for the First Time" and inspired by the birth of my daughter Rebecca in November 1974. I had chosen my graduate program well. Early on, we students were told to select a dissertation topic of particular importance to our lives—nothing arcane or irrelevant to the world at large. Nor were our theses to be statistically fancy and hence likely to gather dust on the graduate library shelf. I remember being most grateful, for I was a statistical neophyte and an insufferable pragmatist.

I was also an expectant father for the first time. My wife was newly pregnant, and our child was due to come into the world sometime during the second semester of school. Lightened by this unanticipated freedom to explore a personally meaningful subject of my own choosing, I skipped off to the medical school library and proceeded to collect reams of documentation on pregnancy studies. I was on my way!

Weeks later, when it came time to present my thesis topic to the class, I enthusiastically announced my well-thought-out plan to create a unique study—one in which, rather than test or question pregnant women, I would interview them. Instead of being "subjects," they would be "participants." I would follow each woman through her pregnancy, birth, and first year of being a parent, trying to capture the mysterious process of expectant motherhood.

Hearing myself talk so animatedly about the project and realizing the vigor with which I was pursuing my research, I couldn't help but remember my zeal some ten years earlier when, having just obtained my driver's license, I implored my father to allow me to drive my pregnant mother to the hospital to give birth to my sister Lori. He complied; I was amazed.

In the midst of my reverie about this early fascination with birth, I was jolted back to my graduate classroom, where my chairperson was commenting, "Jack, you know, you've shown us a wealth of material that is already out there on expectant motherhood. What about expectant fatherhood?" Caught unaware, I was embarrassed. I had never even considered the obvious; here I was, an expectant father myself, yet I had not thought to investigate expectant fatherhood.

Recovering from my embarrassment, I found myself in the grip of anxiety: if I chose to study expectant fatherhood, I would have to come face-to-face with *my own process*. I was caught in a trap of my own making!

I flashed on the words of one of my wisest mentors: "Anxiety is excitement that doesn't know where to go." That pearl of wisdom did the trick. I knew where I had to go, and so with great trepidation and some modicum of curiosity, I accepted the challenge of researching the question: If women are pregnant, could men be too?

I owe much thanks to my professor and classmates for encouraging me to tread what was then the road less traveled, and to the many brave expectant fathers who, traveling with me, lifted me out of denial and into a fuller awareness of myself and my call to fatherhood. Their openness and willingness to explore new vistas inspired within me an urge for self-exploration, an appreciation of the fathering process, and a now long-held desire to help awaken the father in men of all ages.

The book based on my dissertation, *Pregnant Fathers,* appeared in 1982. Then came a barrage of critiques and accusations: Are men really *pregnant?* Doesn't this wording detract from the *woman's* experience? Why undermine the importance of the father by somehow making him the same as the mother? Why are you so fixated on the man's experience, anyway?

After considerable soul-searching, interesting excursions into collective unconscious considerations (Did womb envy predate penis envy?), and much personal reflection (Did I really want to be a psychologist, or was I defending against deeply repressed longings to be an obstetrician, or perhaps the client of one?), I concluded the following: I had used the term "pregnant fathers" not to be cute or to imply that a woman's pregnancy is not hers alone, that the father should be the spotlight of attention during pregnancy, or that the woman should concentrate primarily on her partner, who may be feeling left out of the pregnancy process. Instead, I had chosen the word *pregnant* to illuminate a hidden truth that many people, including myself, had been unaware of—namely, that men entering fatherhood, although not physiologically pregnant, do undergo a profound transformation in personal identity as well as significant psychological changes. My strong hunch was that these dimensions of the male experience must be addressed and understood lest men continue to remain onlookers in the unfolding drama of childbirth, out of touch with their own passage into fatherhood and perhaps unaware of the enormous importance of being involved with their newborns.

This second edition of the book was inspired by the birth of my son Jesse in 1989. The title of this edition is also *Pregnant Fathers,* although the subtitle and entire text have been redrafted. Dreams don't die easily. I hope now, more than ever before, to encourage and support men on their journeys into fatherhood, to highlight the many parallel issues affecting *both* expectant partners, and to further broaden our notions about being pregnant, giving birth, and growing through parenthood. Only in this way, I believe, can we truly appreciate our shared existence as cocreators and as parents capable of giving our children the care, understanding, and love that they so fervently seek and so desperately need in our world.

Lexicographers need not be alarmed. The limiting definition of pregnancy ("being with child") can easily be expanded to incorporate the word's richer nuances ("filled or abounding"; "fertile, rich, full of meaning or possibility"; "highly significant"; "teeming with ideas and imagination"). And while we're at it, let's expand our pitifully inadequate definition of father from "one who begets a child" to:

> one who engages with a child through strength, warmth, tenderness, and understanding, and in the process creates opportunities for personal healing and self-renewal sufficient to awaken the wisdom and sense of purpose needed to bequeath this legacy to the child.

The traditional prescription for good fathering was straightforward: work hard (outside the house), protect the family, plan for the future, and teach right from wrong (through discipline). A father who performed these tasks with regularity and consistency could feel reasonably assured that he was doing his "job" and would earn the love and respect of his wife, children, and community. *We were those children.* And while we may have benefited from our fathers' efforts to provide and protect, we were surely hampered by the shortcomings of the old fathering formula. How many of us have known our fathers man to man or have many memories of candid father-son talks, reassuring hugs, or words of praise and encouragement?

As fathers now ourselves, we are striving for more encompassing relationships with our sons and daughters. In our attempts to create more satisfying fathering roles for ourselves and our children, we are seeking *balance, close emotional contact, hands-on meaningful time with our families, sharing, sensitivity, self-expression,* and *depth.* We are breaking new ground, and we should be proud of our efforts.

To infuse ourselves with new father images and do it well, we must start at the beginning, during pregnancy. This is virgin territory for most men. Neither our grandfathers nor our fathers spoke much about it. We do not carry our children within, and hence have no physiological cues to rely on, no way of accessing information about the intrauterine world. Even so, we can establish deep and rewarding bonds with our children long before they are born. And that is what this book is for.

Throughout these pages, you will find anecdotes from dozens of men and women. You will also find questions to help sharpen your awareness of your underlying attitudes, feelings, and needs, as well as exercises to help you communicate more clearly and effectively with your loved ones. As you read, please pause to contemplate statements or reactions that are significant to you. Take note of your responses, reflect on them, and discuss them with your partner.

Although the two of you are bound to have individual responses to pregnancy and new parenthood, you will happily discover that you also have many responses in common. Your similarities *and* your differences are to be honored. I sincerely hope that the following pages will help shake loose some prenatal misconceptions; help you enjoy unforeseen aspects of your pregnancy, your partnership, and yourselves; and inspire you to communicate so effectively with each other that you enter the wonder of parenthood together, arm in arm and heart to heart. Much joy!

*In creating a child, we invest all that we
are in a future.*

—Paul Brenner

CHAPTER 1

INTRODUCING THE PREGNANT FATHER

When I think back on the pregnancy, I realize that it took me quite a while to realize that I, too, was somehow pregnant. My changes were much more subtle than hers, but undeniably real. I think I started becoming a father right after I heard the news. I know I have been on a voyage of my own. I guess I still am. I am a father now, and somehow I will never be quite the same as before.

PREGNANCY, ESPECIALLY A FIRST PREGNANCY, sets in motion a series of dramatic changes for a woman. Physically, she may feel slight "tugs" and "twinges." Conceptually, she may begin thinking of herself as a bearer of new life, a vessel of sorts. In response, she begins preparing for her transition to motherhood.

All the while, mothers of all ages, eager to share their pregnancy experiences with her, ask her how she is doing and offer emotional support. Even strangers present tips on prenatal health care, feedback on childbirth education classes, and lists of books to read. She soon learns to anticipate sensations ranging from fatigue to nausea and to expect mood fluctuations, anxiety, and vulnerability, as well as a truly altered sense of her body and identity. Her partner also comes to expect these changes in her, considering them an essential part of her transformation to motherhood.

The woman's ultimate adjustment to pregnancy will depend on several factors: the responses and bolstering she receives from friends and family, her general state of health, and her feelings about becoming a mother. She will find relief in knowing that many of her experiences, as unfamiliar and difficult as they may be, can be discussed freely and confirmed by others.

But what about the prospective father? What is happening to him? What is *he* experiencing? What are *his* needs? How does he fit into the picture?

Confessions of a Pregnant Father

I doubt that I would have given these questions much attention before the birth of my first child were it not for my graduate school chairperson and some of my clients and friends. I remember feeling tired and irritable one evening while leading a men's group. Bill, sitting across the room from me, commented that I seemed to be "off somewhere else." Tom, a father of two young children, added that I seemed less energetic than usual. He asked if I was stressed by the pregnancy and remarked, "Fatherhood can sure take a lot out of a guy, you know."

Both comments caught me off guard. Previously, I had been aware only of feeling interested in—and sometimes bewildered by—the changes taking place in my pregnant wife. The idea that the pregnancy might be influencing *me* had never crossed my mind! That the pregnancy could be putting a strain on me made little sense. After all, *she* was pregnant. *She* was the one going through all the changes. It was "business as usual" for me, or so I thought.

As I was driving home that evening, Tom's words came drifting back to me. The implication was that *I* might be having some difficulty adjusting to parenthood and that my lack of vigor was nothing to be defensive about—that I was even *entitled* to feel flustered by the pregnancy. His message, combined with the group's sincere interest and concern, touched me and moved me to look within.

I soon realized that although our pregnancy had been confirmed five months earlier, only now was I able to recognize my own pregnancy experiences. It felt good having my paternity acknowledged and getting some attention for it. I was beginning to see that I was going through an important and perhaps difficult transition of my own: I was *becoming a father.*

Excited by these realizations, I started to let my guard down. I began paying more attention to my thoughts and feelings about becoming a father. I became more mindful of my reactions to the changes going on around me, especially in my wife and our relationship.

Looking back over the previous months, I saw that I had grown somewhat detached from my friends, had been feeling less sociable than usual, and was having trouble concentrating on my work. At home, I was getting into the habit of staying up late, watching old movies, and stuffing myself with junk food. I had also become more temperamental and less decisive than usual, complaining and demanding at the slightest provocation. I reluctantly admitted to myself that I was experiencing tinges of jealousy, too, envying all the attention my wife was getting as well as her unique ability to feel our unborn child moving within her. Sometimes I felt frustrated and crowded in her presence, wanting to be left alone; at other times, I felt uneasy and melancholic and wanted her beside me.

As the weeks passed, I began focusing on the responsibilities I would have to my child and new family. I questioned my motives and aptitudes: Why did I want to be a father? Was I up to the task? Could I be a good provider? Some days, I wished we had postponed the pregnancy until I was more established in my career, older, or wiser. Secretly, I admitted that hearing the news of the pregnancy and feeling the baby move had not really been my idea of exhilaration. The more I reflected, the more I realized how far I was from being the proud, joyful, and enthusiastically anticipating father I thought I would be.

This new awareness upset me a great deal. It didn't seem right for me, a person who sincerely enjoyed children and wanted to have a child, to be harboring such "negative" feelings. Disappointed and confused, I decided to keep the dilemma to myself, afraid that sharing it with my wife would somehow pull us apart. This was a big mistake. To make matters worse, I concluded that I was a neurotic expectant father—that my reactions were unusual, exaggerated, and unwarranted. Surely, I reasoned, if such responses to fatherhood were normal, I would have heard or read about them by now.

Prompted by both concern for my psychological welfare and desire to lay a firm groundwork for my thesis, I searched the local libraries and bookstores for literature on men's reactions to the approach of fatherhood—a quest that proved exceedingly frustrating. The few references I found to expectant fathers were passages in books and articles about expectant motherhood. The portions oriented to male readers explained what pregnancy was like for *women* and how men could be more sensitive and responsive to *them*. Determined to get the inside story, I decided to go directly to the source: expectant fathers themselves.

I spent the next few months talking with expectant fathers about their pregnancy experiences. Most of their initial responses to pregnancy were similar to Steve's: "I'm not really sure what I feel about things. My thoughts and feelings about being a father are all jumbled up. They flee in and out . . . here and gone." As our pregnancies progressed, we became better able to get a grip on our thoughts and feelings about impending fatherhood. Soon we were articulating them and sharing them comfortably with one another. Although we each had our own concerns and ways of coping with them, the themes that emerged were essentially the same: uncertainty, frustration, isolation, anxiety, and hopeful anticipation.

I was not alone after all. In due course, I realized that I was *not* a neurotic father—just a pregnant one!

The Masculine Mythos

Why do we, as men, so often disregard, devalue, and deny our responses to pregnancy? Why don't we instead *acknowledge* them, *express* them, and *welcome* them as elements essential to our passage into fatherhood? Above all, why don't we perceive them as *basic expressions of our masculinity?* The answers to these gnawing questions are embedded in the industrial-age thinking that has dominated Western culture for the past 150 years and in the warrior ethic that has reigned for centuries.

Man, the Laborer. In the 1840s and 1850s, hordes of homesteading men left their families for the factories, where a new assembly-line, productivity-driven ethic was born. Generations of fathers passed on to their sons industry-cast formulas for success, often in the form of injunctions: *Be strong* (Don't let your feelings get in the way of the work), *Don't be so emotional* (Stop acting like a sissy—be a man), *Keep your problems to yourself,* (Keep the wheels of progress spinning), *Stay on top of things* (Be productive and in control at all times), and *Use your head* (Think, solve, achieve).

Striving to "get the job done at all costs" for so long, too many men have lost sight of the enormous price they have paid. A large number of men in our culture have become strangers to their innermost feelings, their need for deep and satisfying relationships, and their essential *being*. We have gotten so far off track that we are out of touch with ourselves and our loved ones. In truth, we are not *what we do;* we are *who we are.* And we will never obtain love or identity from devotion to our jobs, external acclaim, or accomplishment.

Only recently has society begun to champion parenting as a venture shared by mothers *and* fathers. Fathers now routinely participate in childbirth classes, attend the birth of their babies, and visit their newborns in the nursery. Fathers change diapers, read bedtime stories, walk the halls at night, and wear baby carriers. Even so, many men who express nurturing qualities with their little ones see themselves as "mothering" rather than "fathering" and are viewed by others as "good mothers."

The coparenting venture we as a culture strive to implement will remain an impossible ideal until we begin to regard not only parenting but *pregnancy* as a shared undertaking. A world that welcomes the blossoming mother-to-be while disregarding the less visibly blossoming father-to-be inadvertently pushes him out of the picture at the very beginning. And too often, there he stays, an outsider tentative in his attempts to join in the pregnancy and, later, engage with his newborn.

We must begin asking men about *their* pregnancy experiences, about their thoughts, feelings, and dreams of fatherhood. We need to understand that for men, the passage to parenthood is acknowledged primarily through association—"Oh, and *you* must be the proud *father!*" Adding insult to injury, we count on the expectant father to set aside his burgeoning feelings so that he can be diligently attentive to his partner. While adjusting to the many abrupt changes in his routine and his partnership, he dare not complain or be needy himself. Societal expectations of this sort can leave even the best-intentioned father feeling unappreciated, neglected, and frustrated in his attempts to bond in a personal and lasting way with his developing child.

Our pregnancy conventions provide men with neither the validation nor the rites needed to feel included in the transition to parenthood. Although expectant fathers are now welcome guests at prenatal visits, baby showers, and birthing rooms, they have no recognized rituals of their own to guide them into fatherhood and no "community of fathers" to turn to for sustenance. As a result, a man may conclude that he has no alternative but to take a backseat to the unfolding events of pregnancy and infant care, perpetuating his image as a bystander and his feelings of alienation.

Our media trends are no more evolved. Despite soaring numbers of books, films, and TV shows about fathers, *information about fatherhood* is sorely lacking. Fathers are still depicted primarily in their occupational roles, accentuating their accomplishments away from the family rather than their contributions to the quality of family life.

Or they are portrayed at home and perfect in every way. Dr. Huxtable, the modern Hollywood father played by Bill Cosby, is ever available, helpful, involved with his wife and children, and presumably with his patients as well. His home environment suggests that he is also an excellent provider. Thoroughly enamored of this new American father image, we may momentarily forget that we never see him working to earn a living, struggling to balance career with family and personal needs, or endeavoring to maintain an intimate coparenting relationship with his wife. Huxtable is entertainment, not life.

So where are our models of genuine, well-balanced fathers for young men to emulate? Sadly, they are all too rare and hard to find. A society that has for at least 150 years banished its men to the labor force has become a society unable to present more than a fractured father image.

Hollywood aside, we know more about father deprivation than we do about father participation. Nearly half of our children spend a portion of their childhood in a home without a father. Fatherless young men, overly dependent on their mothers while desperately seeking male acceptance and approval, are driven to compulsive, exaggerated, overcompensatory masculine behaviors. Sixty percent of America's rapists, 72 percent of adolescent murderers, and 70 percent of long-term prison inmates grew up without a father.[1]

Individually and collectively, we are paying an exorbitant price for refusing to integrate man-the-worker with man-the-nurturer. Ours is a society replete with absentee fathers (male self-alienation), homophobia (self-rejection), vandalism and theft (emptiness), gang-related crime (search for acceptance), depression and suicide (isolation and self-destructiveness), and acts of violence and brutality (parent-hate and self-loathing). Indeed, the absence of committed, responsible, involved fathers may well be the number one contributor to our most pressing social problems.

The "distant father," "phantom father," and "abusive father" we hear about daily are all products of a culture that does not prepare men to be fathers, or even teach men that nurturing is an essential part of their nature and that *fatherhood is a supreme celebration of manhood*. Without solid ground to stand on, men cannot possibly regard paternity as offering *them* anything of value, accounting in part for why men run from or remain remote and detached from family life.

Man, the Warrior. In his book *Fire in the Belly*, philosopher Sam Keen states that to understand the deep hurt and anger that underlie male violence in America, we must recognize that men's psyches have been shaped by another cultural expectation—that males must be prepared to suffer, die, and kill to protect those they love. A succession of generations was raised on a man-at-arms ethic that went something like this: "To support his family, the man has to be distant, away hunting or fighting wars; to be tender, he must be tough enough to fend off enemies. To be generous, he must be selfish enough to amass goods, often by defeating other men; to be gentle, he must first be strong, even ruthless in confronting enemies; to love, he must be aggressive enough to court, seduce, and 'win' a wife."[2] This warrior aspect of manhood, Keen reminds us, evolved not out of an inherent heartlessness or predilection for cruelty, but

out of historical necessity. For centuries, men were called upon to muscle their way through life.

And the beat goes on. In today's "enlightened" era, we are raising our boys to aspire to wealth, success, and power in the business world, or to make their mark on the professional community, rather than to be creative and emotionally present as fathers, friends, and lovers. While little girls may play house, cradling dolls and rehearsing at being mommy, most little boys persist in playing out traditional masculine roles with knock-'em-dead electronics, competitive games, guns of all shapes and sizes, and endless quantities of sports paraphernalia. (And when a little boy doesn't gravitate toward these activities, we worry about his sexual identity.)

Our sons are still not experiencing much touch, comfort, and nurturing from their fathers. Boys who demonstrate patience, sensitivity, and empathy are all too often learning to do so from their mothers, grandmothers, or teachers, not their fathers.

William's Doll, an award-winning children's book by Charlotte Zolotow, portrays such a boy. William is an ordinary four year old who wants nothing more than to hug, feed, swing, dress, and read goodnight books to his little, hoped-for girl doll. His brothers and the boy next door mock him. His father sets out on a campaign to interest him in "boy" games. And although William becomes quite skilled at basketball and enjoys his electric trains, he—much to his father's dismay—does not stop wanting a doll.

One day, William's grandmother comes for a visit, and as they walk together into the countryside, he tells her of his longing for a doll. She listens and smiles with understanding and approval. The next day, she buys William just the doll he has wanted. To his distraught father, she explains: "He needs it, to hug and to cradle and to take to the park so that when he's a father like you, he'll know how to take care of his baby and feed him and love him and bring him the things he wants, like a doll so that he can practice being a father."[3]

The warrior ethic has dominated far too long. It is time to create a new vocabulary for masculinity, words and phrases that can lead men back to themselves. Author and columnist Richard Louv, for example, has recently coined the term "fatherman." He states, and I concur, "Men will not move back into the family until our culture reconnects masculinity and fatherhood, until young men come to see fatherhood, not just paternity, as the fullest expression of manhood"—until a young man knows that he can be a "fatherman" who can give "fatherlove."[4] We are sorely in need of a working definition of manhood that blends strength with gentleness and brings together the good fathering we received with the fathering we needed and longed for. It is time to declare that masculinity has everything to do with fathering.

Our Fathers, Ourselves. The old mythos lives on because a new, more balanced image of fathering has not yet taken root. Boys learn about fathering primarily through working and playing with their fathers and by watching their fathers with others, yet relatively few fathers of the past generation have spent significant amounts of focused, continuous time with their sons. As Cat Stevens laments in his song "Father and Son": "How can I try to explain, 'cause when I do he [Father] turns away again. / It's always been the same old story: from the moment I could talk, I was ordered to listen. . . . / All the times that I've cried, keeping all the things I knew inside. / It's hard, but it's harder to ignore it. / If they were right, I'd agree, but it's them they know, not me. / Now there's a way, and I know that I have to go away. I know I have to go."[5]

The "provider father"—who provides for the family's physical and material well-being at the expense of proffering his love and accessibility—is the most pervasive image for men of our times. No wonder today's busy father, whether he is an overworked CEO or a laborer juggling three jobs, is so often too tired or distracted to recognize that his children are, like himself, following in the footsteps of the father they know. Harry Chapin, songwriter and storyteller, drives this tragic dynamic home in his song "Cat's in the Cradle." Chapin sings of a young boy who asks, "When you coming home, Dad?" and his father's reply, "I don't know when. But we'll be together then. You know we'll have a good time then." Years later, when the boy comes home from college and borrows the keys to the car, his father asks, "When you coming home, son?" The boy replies: "I don't know when. But we'll get together then, Dad. You know we'll have a good time then." Years later, when the father calls his son, requesting, "I'd like to see you if you don't mind," the son, now a father himself, replies, "I'd love to, Dad, if I can find the time. . . ."[6]

Our parents' behavior has left a deep and lasting impression on us. For better or worse, intentionally or inadvertently, we tend to replay with our children the type of parenting we received—until we scrupulously examine our motives, values, behavior, and intentions, and consciously strive to avoid the mistakes our parents made. Herein lies the hope. We need only be clear, brave, and persistent enough to proceed.

Reconceiving Fatherhood

Men today are expected to assume responsibility for child care and household chores; to display nurturing behavior; to be sensitive, self-aware, and expressive of their feelings; and to provide materially for the health and welfare of their families. Fathers of the nineties must also cope with the practical and psychological aspects of a two-career household, recession or inflation, and geographic separation from their families and communities of origin. In short, they must fulfill fathering roles that they never learned, never even saw in action. Today's father must create a unique vision of fatherhood for himself and his children—one that incorporates an image of men as potent nurturers *within* the family as well as effective connectors with the world *outside* the family.

Becoming a new kind of father is the most challenging task a man can undertake. When pursued with heart, it may well be his most rewarding life accomplishment. Family therapist John B. Franklin calls the process of becoming a father "fatherbirth" and explains that this, like childbirth, incorporates change, anxiety, risk-taking, and work, "and brings with it all the uncertainty, labor, frustration, and joy that invariably accompany change."[7] Giving birth to *ourselves as fathers,* we discard a borrowed lifestyle, forge a new identity, and embrace the promise of continued growth.

Reconceiving fatherhood takes much more than desire. Peter, who is having a hard time deepening his relationship with his newborn, explains his impasse this way: "The feeling that just flashed on me is that mothers are closer to children than fathers. I guess I'm jealous of that. I want to be as close to my child as my wife is. Yet [and here's the glitch] there's a biological tie that I'm sure develops. I don't feel as strongly for my father as I do for my mother, and I think that's bound up in the feelings that mothers and children have for each other, something qualitatively different from what a man can have for his child and the child for his father." Peter, like many newcomers to fatherhood, would like to be more intimately involved with his infant, yet lacks perspective and confidence. Myths and misconceptions are holding him back from being all he can be.

To re-create fatherhood, three qualities are needed: *vision* expansive enough to see what is important for our children and our world, *thought* penetrating enough to dispel a multitude of erroneous and long-outdated viewpoints, and *courage* steadfast enough to bind us to our convictions. The day has come for not only fathers, but mothers, grandparents, educators, health providers, and policymakers to break through old biases and together create a world in which our children can thrive.

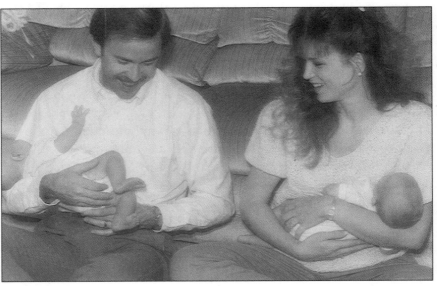

Suzanne Arms

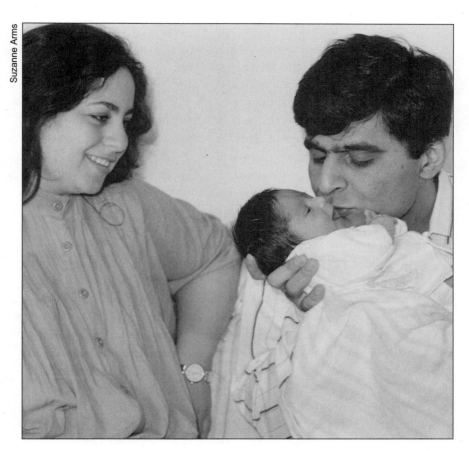

Suzanne Arms

Let's begin by setting the record straight:

- *Parenting is not a sex-linked trait.* A vast quantity of research indicates that motivated fathers are as sensitive to infant behavior as mothers are, and as competent at reading newborn cues and nurturing babies. Moreover, the desire to parent is as intrinsic to men as it is to women. Parenting is, in final analysis, a fundamental way of *being* with another person—a way of conveying affection and understanding, of transmitting beliefs and values, and of relating beyond ourselves through acceptance, committed involvement, and love.

- *Newborns have no innate preference for one parent over the other.* Babies form powerful emotional attachments with both mother and father—as well as with adoptive and foster parents, grandparents, and siblings. Bonding is established through abundant skin-to-skin, face-to-face, loving contact during the first hours and days of life. Although a newborn's initial attachment figure is usually the mother, many infants respond to their fathers with cooing, smiling, and signs of excitement. Infants also form primary attachments to their fathers.

- *Effective parenting is synergistic, and babies reap the rewards.* A father's involvement with his newborn in no way diminishes the importance of the mother's role. In fact, when fathers are supportive partners and involved caretakers, their infants are likely to establish a secure maternal attachment *and* a secure paternal attachment. Fathers who feel supported and encouraged by their partners, compared with those who do not, are more comfortable and confident parenting their infants. Similarly, mothers who feel supported and encouraged by their partners feel more competent and responsive to their children and often have easier labors and births. Infants whose parents communicate meaningfully and parent well together get to interact with *two* sources of love.[8]

- *Fathers have a profound and lasting effect on their infants' development.* Children who experience involved fathering are more likely than others to develop creative, intellectual, and social skills; decrease their vulnerability to psychological problems; and establish a positive body image, gender security, self-esteem, and moral strength.[9]

- *Children grow best when mothers and fathers share parenting responsibilities while respecting each other's differences and supporting each other's efforts.* Shared parenting conveys to the child an emotional commitment from both parents, which in turn fosters a sense of trust and security, acceptance and confidence, and curiosity and eagerness to explore.[10]

Suzanne Arms

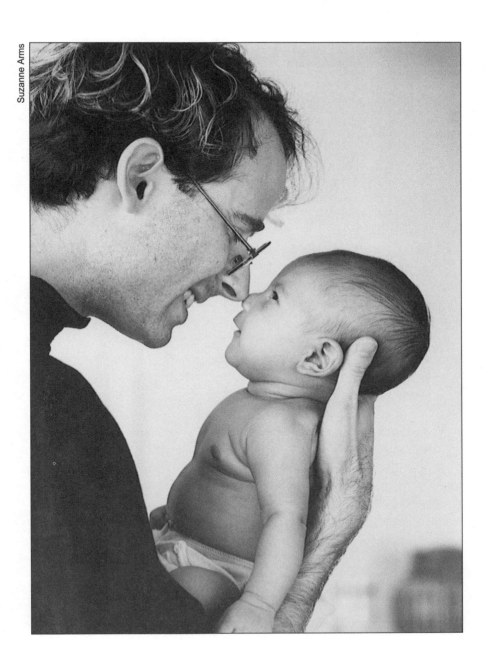

If you bottle up your feelings . . . eventually they'll all go sour.

—Ashleigh Brilliant

CHAPTER 2

A GOOD LOOK AT FEELINGS AND NEEDS

Looking back, I'm not sure I could put words to what I was feeling. I know I didn't want to impose my moods on her or even let her know I was having some uncomfortable feelings. I never much liked having to ask, for anything . . . it's easier to take care of these kinds of things myself.

EXPECTANT FATHERS AND MOTHERS are often understandably uncomfortable with the shifting emotions of pregnancy. Having to wait nine months for the baby's arrival certainly compounds the difficulty. You need not sit back, however, and be buffeted by the turbulence. Instead, you can venture in and explore all that pregnancy has to offer. Those who have confirm that there is no more valuable journey one can take.

I have learned from both my own experience and my work with other parents that a fulfilling psychological voyage depends on two essential factors. One is a partner who is nearby, available, and willing to share the journey. The second is time. Every worthwhile excursion takes time, and this one takes plenty—to access the terrain, to chart a personally tailored course of travel, and to glean insights each step of the way.

Taking In the Emotional Landscape

How aware are you in general of your emotional reactions to others? What feelings do you experience most often when you are with friends, your partner, your parents? When and how do you express *pleasant* feelings (happiness, comfort, serenity, caring, enthusiasm,

A WORLD

Uncertain   Hopeful   Confused

Nervous   Afraid   Empathetic   Vulnerable

Withdrawn   Hurt   Loving   Comforting

Amazed   Hesitant   Worried   Lonely

OF FEELINGS

Envious   Contented   Trapped   Angry

Resentful   Tender   Safe   Anticipating   Determined

Relieved   Overwhelmed   Proud

Playful   Delighted

pride, excitement, passion)? When and how do you express *unpleasant* feelings (hurt, jealousy, sadness, anger)?

What happens when you censor yourself? Do you take your suppressed emotions out on *others* by being moody, impatient, or blaming? Do you take them out on *yourself* and become tense, tired, self-critical, or depressed?

With whom are you most comfortable sharing yourself? Why is this so? With whom are you least comfortable? Why? What do you imagine would happen if you told these people how you really feel and what you would really like from them? What is keeping you from expressing yourself more freely?

How aware we are of our feelings, the way we express them, and our sense of which ones are "OK" were all learned in childhood. Dependent on our caretakers for attention, love, and guidance, we made early decisions about what "works" in our interactions with others. If smiling elicited hugs, we smiled, regardless of our actual feelings. If being "good," smart, unselfish, quiet, or outgoing elicited approval, we mastered these traits. Even when all we could hope for was to avoid punishment or rejection, we quickly learned that it was worth our while to do the "right thing."

As adults, we tend to repeat these patterned responses with people we care about, unaware that we are sharing our "conditioned" selves rather than our real selves. To become "present," or emotionally available, to those we love, we must take a good, hard look at the emotional lessons we learned—and didn't learn—while growing up.

Clearing Away the Overgrowth

When we were young, our parents were our gods and goddesses. What they told us about life was unquestionably true. Eager to please them, and to master the mysterious world around us, we paid close attention to their spoken and unspoken messages, adopting their perceptions and values as our own.

ANOTHER LOOK AT MOM AND DAD

Picture your mother's face for a moment, or visualize a childhood scene with her in it. What feelings was she (wasn't she) displaying? Did you usually experience her as happy, sad, angry, distressed? Did she talk about her feelings? If so, how? Try the same exercise, thinking about your dad.

Now picture your parents together. How did this scene feel to you then—warm, relaxed, tense? Were your parents looking at each other, listening to each other, or paying lip service to each other? Did they show their caring? If so, how—by listening, smiling, touching, kissing, laughing, getting angry? How did your parents most often communicate their feelings and wants *to* each other, and *for* each other? Did they talk, touch, argue? Did they make small talk or discuss important concerns and feelings? Did they seem to trust each other with their true desires? How did they convey this? Did they talk behind each other's back?

Next, picture each of your parents *with you* as a child. How were you comforted and disciplined?

What conclusions did you draw from your mother and father about emotions, about relationships? Try filling in the following blanks: *Seeing my mother (father, parents)* _____, *I learned* _____ *about love (feelings, wants, marriage, sex roles, parenting, being a child, being an adult).*

Share your discoveries with your partner.

To augment this exercise, use photographs from your childhood and adolescence as a springboard to reverie. Bind up a few for future reference.

Many of us internalized some combination of the following messages:

> "Children (and their feelings and wants) are to be seen and not heard."
>
> "Feelings are a nuisance. They get in the way. They get you in trouble."
>
> "Your parents are always right. They know what's best for you." (They know you better than you know yourself.)
>
> "Don't ask for anything. You'll get what you deserve. Don't be ungrateful. Don't complain. Don't be greedy. Be happy with what you have." (If there's something you don't have, maybe you didn't deserve it.)
>
> "People who love each other don't argue."
>
> "Don't get angry." (People will reject you if you are angry.)
>
> "Don't cry . . . shhh. Be strong." (Don't feel sad, hurt, or upset.)
>
> "Don't be a monster." (Don't ask for attention.)
>
> "Don't interrupt." (We're more important than you are.)
>
> "Don't be selfish." (Put others' needs before your own.)

Fortunate was the child who internalized statements like these:

> "Feelings are natural and good." (What are you feeling?)
>
> "It is all right to talk about your feelings." (Let's discuss it.)
>
> "I care about what you want." (I hear you; I understand.)
>
> "Don't be afraid to speak up." (I'm here beside you; it's safe to talk.)

Whatever your childhood messages were, remember that they are rooted in the *past* and may no longer be suitable. We are now living in a different time, a new place. As adults, we can consciously select the values we *want to* adhere to and cast off the rest.

Our parents also passed down admonitions on how to live in a family as husband and wife, mother and father. The customary axioms—most of which were transmitted by *their* parents—began with:

> "A good husband (wife) should/would _____."
>
> "A good parent should/would _____."

"A good husband (wife) shouldn't/wouldn't _____."
"A good parent shouldn't/wouldn't _____."
"A good child will/will not _____."

Much of this counsel was strongly judgmental and of questionable merit. What *we* strive for as adults may differ radically from what *our parents* expected of themselves as parents and of us as children.

THE VALLEY OF SHOULDS AND SHOULDN'TS

Thinking back on your childhood, list the *shoulds* and *shouldn'ts* you learned about parenting, partnering, loving, giving, asking, and doing. Ask your partner to do the same. (Write quickly, and avoid wondering whether you heard these messages or picked them up by reading between the lines. Trust what comes to mind.)

Compare notes with your partner. How similar were your upbringings? Which recommendations do you currently agree with? Which ones are getting in the way? What can you do about them?

Give voice to your new intentions, and help each other do some emotional filtering.

In addition to childhood injunctions and admonitions, there were prohibitions. Most of us were discouraged from expressing our feelings and needs spontaneously and fully. Consequently, to secure the love and attention we longed for, we resorted to indirect maneuvers. We learned to be "good" and agreeable, accommodating and understanding, overgiving and self-denying, withholding and self-deprecating, aggressive and blaming, or self-conscious and perfectionistic.

We developed a repertoire of relationship tactics—not to be

deceptive, but to ensure our emotional survival in a difficult, perhaps abusive, environment. As children, we discovered that we *had*
to be indirect about our feelings because their direct expression was
frowned upon or forbidden by parents who were either unable to
satisfy them (perhaps they were too needy themselves) or unable to
comprehend them or give personal expression to them. As adults in
today's world, however, we are called upon to respond openly and
directly to those we love. Ironically, the childhood maneuvers that
helped us adjust to life with our *parents* stifle the intimacy we seek
in our *present relationships*.

Now is an excellent time to gather up the old lessons, scrutinize
them, discard those that do not generate joy and meaningful contact with others, and affirm those that reflect your present values.
This is no simple task. Getting to know yourself well enough to live
in congruence with your feelings and beliefs will take determination
and fortitude.

A good way to begin is by becoming solidly familiar with the
emotional facts of life, including the following:

- You are entitled to your feelings. Emotions are not debat-
  able. There are no good, bad, right, wrong, real, or unreal
  feelings—although some are certainly more comfortable
  than others. *Do not belittle or judge any of your feelings.*
- The awareness of feelings paves the way to self-under-
  standing, self-confidence, and closer relationships. The
  direct expression of feelings helps release tension, dissolve
  worries, and invigorate the spirit.
- Unpleasant emotions that are *avoided* or *denied* ("held in")
  fester, leading to stress, alienation, and resentment.
  Avoidance, denial, and other defensive patterns can easily
  become habitual and disruptive in your important relationships. In contrast, unpleasant emotions that are *shared*—
  free of contempt, criticism, or blame—cultivate new and
  enduring communication pathways.
- Feelings that are discounted by others trigger frustration,
  resentfulness, and anger. Turning these emotions inward
  can lead to self-criticism and depression. *Avoid people who
  invalidate your feelings.*

- Feelings are transitory. When aired and accepted, unpleasant feelings will quickly fade.
- Feelings are not black-or-white. It is natural to have ambivalent and contradictory feelings about people and things.

Pregnant Parents' Needs and Rights

Emotional needs become magnified during pregnancy. Yet, caught up in monitoring the medical progress of gestation, preparing for the birth, and planning for the newborn, expectant mothers and fathers commonly overlook their heightened emotional needs. It is vitally important not only to tap in to these emotional vistas, but to give expression to them early on.

Enhanced Emotional Needs. The months of pregnancy can be disorienting, even frightening. As such, this is an especially important time to reach out to friends, relatives, and your partner for multiple doses of the nutrients you ordinarily need to sustain your sense of well-being and enthusiasm for life. At the very least, you will need, in daily dosages:

- To feel accepted and validated—perhaps with a smile, a touch, or a heartfelt "I adore you," "You look wonderful," "You mean so much to me," "I appreciate you," "I've missed you," or "Thanks."
- To feel valued, trusted, and lovable—by receiving an invitation to spend time with a loved one, a request for help, or an offer to share memories, dreams, and reflections. Nothing communicates this message more immediately than a warm embrace, a touch, or the words "I love you. I'm glad you're here with me."
- Support for being yourself—to have opportunities for honest, direct, and deep communication with others.
- To feel safe in knowing that you are loved for who you are (not for pretending, maneuvering, or playing out some role expectation)—to be certain that whatever you feel, do, say, or ask for, your partner's love and caring will continue undiminished.

- To feel understood—to know that someone will take time to listen to your point of view without judging or trying to change you.

The more emotionally secure and fulfilled you feel during pregnancy, the more available and responsive you will be to your partner. And the better equipped you will be to open yourself heart and soul to your child.

Entitlement Questions. Parents-in-waiting often exclaim, "I can't tell her *this!*" or "I can't burden him with *that!*" or "I don't have the *right* to expect such a thing!" During my first pregnancy, for example, I decided not to tell my wife of my ambivalence about taking on fatherhood. It didn't seem fair to overload her with *my* worries. At the time, I didn't realize that underlying my perceived lack of entitlement was a great deal of trepidation about angering her, getting into a fight, being judged, or having her pull away from me.

Contrary to what we may have learned, holding back important thoughts, feelings, needs, and expectations does not spare *anyone* anguish—not our partners, not our friends, and certainly not ourselves. Withholding critical information only creates a wall of inhibition and alienation.

To avoid roadblocking your relationship, try to mutually agree on some basic relationship ground rules. Write them down, and refer to them whenever the need arises. Discuss and edit them freely.

Your agreement may look something like this.

We will support and encourage each other to:
- Be honest.
- Have expectations, feelings, and desires.
- Express emotions naturally. (Be emotional.)
- Ask for what we want and need.
- Make mistakes. (Be imperfect.)
- Be unreasonable and unfair at times.
- Say no.
- Not know. (Say, "I don't know.")
- Not fulfill a request. (Say, "Not right now.")
- Avoid having to justify or explain our actions.
- Be inconsistent, illogical, and irrational.
- Change our minds.

- Not always be responsible.
- Put ourselves first.
- Be afraid.
- Push through our fears.

Parents Are People Too. For generations, mothers have been expected to give their all to childrearing, and fathers have been expected to provide to the max—part of the parenting legacy we have inherited. Assuming that such goals are even attainable, we must question whether or not they are desirable.

Balance is essential. An infant's immediate need for sustenance and nurturance must not obscure the fact that parents need care and attention to sustain *themselves* and *their relationship*.

Pregnancy is an ideal time to reflect on some parental facts of life, such as:

- Parenting does not begin at childbirth. It begins when two individuals first conceive of "wanting to be pregnant" and consciously start making love and forming a union with this intention in mind.
- Parenthood is maturational. We relive our own childhood experiences during each stage of our child's growth. We develop *with* our children, learning more about who we are each step of the way.
- Effective parenting requires a healthy balance between fulfillment *within* the family and *outside* the family.
- Parents' needs and children's needs are not necessarily compatible. Conflicting needs must be taken into account and negotiated regularly.
- Biological parents are not the only people who parent well. Stepparents, adoptive parents, grandparents, godparents, and other loving human beings do too.
- Parents have significant interests beyond parenting. Such pursuits are best added in small increments so that balance will be maintained.
- Parenting both creates and interferes with life opportunities.
- Effective parenting is an acquired skill. We learn it as we go.
- There are many different styles of good parenting.
- Good parents cannot control the outcome of their parenting.

- Parenting tasks are, with few exceptions, interchangeable and negotiable.
- Dissimilar parenting styles do not create conflict-ridden children. Differences are most often an asset. The key is to combine divergent ideas and talents in complementary ways.
- Reciprocity promotes satisfying family relationships.

A further parental fact of life: *fathers are not for sons alone.* A father figures prominently in his daughter's development. Because he represents her first relationship with a male, he becomes her male-ideal, her model of how men behave toward women and children. A daughter's impressions of her father, as well as the lessons she learns in his presence, color and shape her perceptions of herself as a female, of men as partners and fathers, and of male-female relationships.

Songstress and writer Judy Collins recalls the power of her father's love in these lyrics: "My father always promised us that we would live in France. / We'd go boating on the Seine and I would learn to dance. / We lived in Ohio then. He worked in the mines. / On his dreams like boats we knew, we sailed in time. . . . / And I live in Paris now. My children dance and dream. / Hearing the words of a miner's life in worlds they've never seen. / I send my

Michael Weisbrot

memories afar like boats across the Seine / And watch the Paris sun set in my father's eyes again."[11]

Fatherly Ways

Although the role of fathers is in great flux, the qualities of effective fathering are enduring. These qualities live deep within and need only be cultivated—an activity that is best begun during the months of pregnancy.

Here is a checklist of areas to contemplate as you fine-tune your fatherly instincts:

- Protect by being available, receptive, and responsive.
- Provide with awareness, support, consistency, and continuity.
- Access your warmth, sensitivity, and loving feelings. Demonstrate these qualities in deeds; express them generously in words and through touch.
- Teach and guide through acceptance, encouragement, and positive expectations.

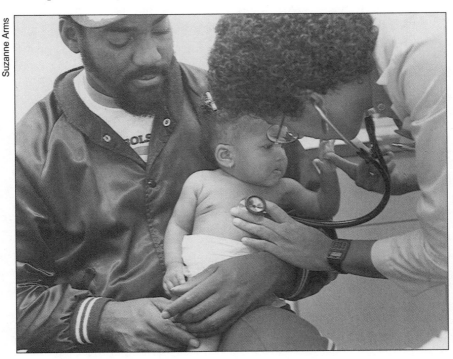

Suzanne Arms

Suzanne Arms

- Model trust and honesty. Say what you mean, mean what you say, and do what you say you'll do.
- Discipline with love. Set limits. Show that unacceptable behavior has logical consequences. Be patient and flexible, firm and sure.
- Cooperate with your partner.
- Strive to know yourself, to examine what has made you the person you are, and to become conscious of your blind spots, your insecurities, and your limits. Be aware of your issues (control, conflict-avoidance, dependency), your fears, and your strengths.
- Practice self-acceptance and gentleness with yourself. Remember that at any given time, you can be only who you are. Avoid perfectionism. Do not push the river; it flows by itself. What you need will be there when you are ready to receive it.
- Steer clear of the need to do, solve, or fix. Life is also about *be*ing. Relax on a regular basis. Let yourself be.[12]

The transition to parenthood is by no means easy. Couples rank pregnancy and early parenting among their most trying periods together. Familiar routines are interrupted. Accustomed ways of sharing and relating often prove inadequate. New responsibilities and priorities emerge. Unanticipated emotions, questions, and concerns surface abruptly. Becoming a parent—aka "really a grown-up"—shakes our perception of ourselves, our partners, our parents, our friends, and our lives. No one remains unruffled in the midst of all this tumult.

The good news is that the shake-up helps us reorganize for the tasks ahead. It awakens the compassion, tolerance, trust, and spirit of cooperation we will need in times to come.

Parenting together challenges couples to develop an especially close working alliance—a mutually enriching union in which three people's feelings, concerns, and needs can be heard and responded to. Parenthood compels us to open to our feelings, find meaningful ways of sharing them, and begin asking for what we want. Parenthood is one of our greatest teachers.

Jill Fineberg

NOURISHING A QUALITY

Take a few slow, deep breaths. Close your eyes, and allow your attention to move from the busyness of the outside world to the rhythm of your breathing or your heartbeat. Let your thoughts slow down; let your body come to rest comfortably, relaxed and receptive.

Picture a scene in which you are holding your child. Notice yourself feeling *at ease* and *content.*

Now imagine yourself experiencing and expressing any quality you wish—tenderness, playfulness, love, freedom, delight. Allow your body to take in the pleasure of being with your child.

Hold in your mind an image of this moment. Concentrate on the sensations you feel. Enjoy them. Absorb them. Claim them as yours. Know that you will be able to recapture this experience anytime you wish.

Drawing from this exercise, compose an affirmation for yourself: *As a father I am _____ (loving, attentive, happy, kind, involved).*

Bring your affirmation to mind often; breathe new life into this treasured moment.

One's feelings are the source of one's energy; they provide the horsepower that makes it possible for us to accomplish the tasks of living. Since they work for us, we should treat them with respect.

—M. Scott Peck

CHAPTER 3

AS FEELINGS AND NEEDS CHANGE

I'm sure that something important is happening to me. There are things going on inside me, I know. But I don't quite have the words for them. Somehow, it's like I'm running around in circles with my thoughts and feelings.

MANY EXPECTANT FATHERS EXPERIENCE A "CLOUDINESS" following the confirmation of pregnancy. And with little wonder. The baby is not yet visible. The mother-to-be seems much the same as always, aside from some vague symptoms that sound very much like an upset stomach or premenstrual cramps. Nothing seems especially out of the ordinary. It is tempting at times to even doubt the results of the pregnancy test, finding the "whole thing" so "unreal" and "hard to fathom."

As Jeff, three months pregnant, explains: "Acknowledging that what was unreal is now suddenly real—that's definitely making a transition. And there is something scary about taking that leap. It means I have to get involved. There are things I must learn and do and feel and take part in. There's a commitment involved here. It's a very heavy thing to be happening. I know it's there, but it hasn't really sunk in yet."

So You Say We're Pregnant?

At this early point in pregnancy, feelings are often beyond reach. When they begin to take shape, an array of responses emerges, including some you may not have expected, such as ambivalence, apprehension, and self-doubt. If you were not "planning on" pregnancy, or were not wanting to conceive a child at this point in your life, your responses may range from disappointment to out-and-out resentment, from apprehension to full-blown fear. For me, the intrusion of uncomfortable feelings in the early months of pregnancy seemed inappropriate; I did not want to entertain these "unwelcome guests." Scores of men report similar reactions, along with confusion, guilt, or anxiety.

If the feelings that surface for you are in any way disagreeable, try not to be alarmed. Despite culturally prescribed "right ways" to feel about being pregnant, a broad range of emotions are elicited by the powerful events unfolding at this time. Take comfort in knowing that whatever your responses are, they will ring true for other fathers as well. Ask them. You may be greatly relieved by what they say.

Ambivalence. Regardless of your perceived "readiness" for this pregnancy, anticipate mixed feelings. No one is on cloud nine all the time, and expectant fathers are no exception. Jim, for example, struggled constantly with his responses to pregnancy. Not until month five of gestation did he realize that his inability to fully accept the pregnancy hinged on self-judgments about his own ambivalence. "I was telling myself it's not OK to not feel perfectly wonderful about everything. You're not supposed to feel part OK and part not OK," he said, then added, "There's something really scary as well as exciting about being in a place you don't know anything about."

The Many Faces of Denial. Unfortunately, expectant fathers are often unwilling to admit to their mixed feelings. Some men bypass them by feigning immediate acceptance of their new parenthood status. Jerry, shaken by an unexpected pregnancy, shared these thoughts soon after hearing the news: "Although it was a surprise, it didn't bother me . . . I was able to completely accept it within probably a week or so . . . It's fine with me that she is pregnant. It won't really upset our plans, although not being able to go camping and other things like that. . . . They're not all that important, after all—especially since we had both decided to have children sometime in the future, anyway." Jerry's long pauses, the tenseness in his voice, and his forced grins conveyed his true feelings: he was disappointed and scared. In acting compulsively fearless, Jerry was denying his true experience and rejecting an important part of himself.

Other men sidestep their ambivalent feelings by focusing exclusively on their pregnant partners. A man who downplays his own experiences may succeed in reducing his anxiety for a while, at least until the pregnancy becomes obvious or the baby begins kicking. Predictably, however, as fatherhood becomes more tangible, conflicted feelings about having a baby become increasingly more difficult to hide.

Still other expectant fathers strive to temper their "undesirable" feelings. As Steve explains: "All along, the major thing I've been trying to do is get rid of the scary parts of what I feel and focus on the positive parts of becoming a father. It's really hard, like fighting a battle with yourself." Steve *is* fighting a battle with himself, one he is destined to lose, for the problem is not his apprehension but his determination to disallow it.

In lieu of tempering unwanted feelings, a pregnant father in denial may try *withholding* (being silent or distant), *accommodating* (being the "perfect" expectant father), *placating* (always saying yes), *blaming* (attributing his feelings or intentions to others), or *displacing* (taking out his feelings on others). These methods, while offering temporary relief, greatly increase stress levels. The accumulated tension invariably erupts in aggressive outbursts, depression, or physical illness either during pregnancy or soon afterward.

By disallowing his feelings—attempting to *do* something with them rather than simply *accept* them—an expectant father withdraws emotionally and physically from his partner. Feeling abandoned and having no way to understand his behavior, *she* is apt to mistake his unavailability for a waning interest in her or their unborn baby. A vicious cycle ensues: the more distant and unapproachable he becomes, the more likely she is to feel hurt and resentful, and to respond with aloofness herself. Displays of affection soon subside, whereupon lovemaking and intimacy may become a distant memory.

Denial, in its many guises, not only impedes the flow of marital communication and loving exchange but breeds serious and lasting side effects. Long-lingering feelings of frustration, resentment, and isolation do not evaporate as birth draws near and are not easily resolved afterward, when attention turns naturally to parental responsibilities. Nor is the birth experience itself immune to their impact.

Jerry, whose wife's physical discomfort and medical complications kept them homebound much of the time, never admitted that he was having difficulty adjusting to pregnancy. Whenever we spoke, he emphasized Nancy's troubles, liberally sprinkling his commentary with *wes*. Rarely did he say *I,* and not once did he mention his *own* reactions to becoming a parent.

Jerry and Nancy went to childbirth classes together, and Jerry attended the birth of his child. When Carla was born, Jerry gazed at her face and was shocked. "My immediate reaction was, 'This is something very strange,'" he recalls. "She didn't look like a living thing . . . just a wriggly, rubbery thing. It didn't seem right, somehow. She didn't seem to belong to me, or be part of me. She was kind of a stranger. I couldn't make the connection between her and me." In truth, *Jerry* was the stranger—a stranger to himself and therefore to his newborn. The ambivalent feelings he had so actively denied for nine months surfaced at the most inopportune moment imaginable, jolting him into a staggering sense of estrangement, and later, depression.

Fortunately, Jerry entered counseling and gradually developed a wonderful closeness with Carla. Nevertheless, he is not likely to ever forget the mortifying moment of his daughter's birth.

Self-Doubt, Guilt, Uncertainty. In the early stages of pregnancy, men are apt to undergo periods of self-doubt, in part because so much is expected of them—more than ever before. Seeing themselves falling short of role ideals, they may believe they have committed a breach of conduct. Guilt-ridden, they may develop qualms about their future performance. As Paul, a newly expectant father, says: "There was something reprehensible about the fact that I felt laid back when I found out she was pregnant, that I didn't feel inspired, happy, and overjoyed. Actually, I was tied up with some frightening feelings."

If you, like Paul, feel guilty or disappointed in yourself for falling short of expectations, remember that waiting in the wings alongside your difficult feelings are your joy, satisfaction, pride, and eager anticipation. Know, too, that they will wait there until you open the door to *all* the emotions you are experiencing. Whenever one emotion is censored, all others become blocked. So give expression to whatever is there. The way out is not *around,* but *through.*

Your partner can help by clarifying *her* needs and expectations ("I'd like some more time with you") and by sharing her own concerns about becoming a parent ("I feel unsure of myself too"). Most of all, *you* can help—by talking about your changes with her and with friends. Start early. You will be pleasantly surprised to see how quickly a little articulation can clear the pathways to communication.

We Certainly *Are* Pregnant!

When pregnancy is confirmed, a man knows in his mind that he is a father; only later can he know it in his heart and soul. As Miguel explains, eight months into pregnancy: "Each little experience is like pounding a nail while building a home. The beginning of the construction was when we first found out she was pregnant. I was very far away from being a father then. Yet, each of the experiences that followed was like another hit on the nail, another wall framed, then a room . . . hammering it all home. My fatherhood is becoming stronger and more solid with each one of these experiences, and so am I. I'm really quite comfortable with the whole thing now—finally."

Financial Responsibility. As pregnancy progresses, you will no doubt encounter a new sense of financial responsibility. The father-as-provider role still looms large, especially for men with fluctuating incomes, tenuous job security, or earnings that appear insufficient to accommodate a new family member. Providing financially also takes on urgency for men who are unaccustomed to being the sole supporter of the family.

Economic concerns are perfectly natural, particularly in a nation that offers no child allowance, no paid parental leave, no guaranteed health insurance, and no large-scale housing subsidies for families. Warren, recently married and now pregnant and laid off from his job, is anxiously seeking employment as a handyman. He describes his concerns this way: "I've been feeling nervous off and on. I'm sure it has something, maybe a lot, to do with the financial pressures of being a dad. It's one thing to think about going through hard times by myself. But this baby has basically nothing. I have a responsibility to make sure my wife and child are taken care of."

Emotional Responsibility. Pregnancy catapults you out of the present and—ready or not—into the future. Seemingly mundane activities suddenly assume new meaning. Simple, everyday decisions take on major implications. Don't be surprised to find yourself suddenly reevaluating your goals, beliefs, strengths, and weaknesses. As disconcerting as these shifts can be, they move you along major trails on the pathway to parenthood. Try to welcome each new vista as an opportunity for personal and relationship growth.

Lee, midway through pregnancy and concerned about how effective he will be as a father, has initiated a self-improvement program. He relates: "I'm doing more to help myself be the best person I can be. I'm watching my diet and working out more. I'm trying to be more decisive, less wishy-washy. I'm reading some and thinking more about my new family and the influence my actions are going to have *on my child.* All this is affecting my power of concentration, changing my focus—for the better, I'm sure."

Tony, whose father was seldom home or available to him as a child, is reflecting on the kind of father he wants to be. "I'm thinking a lot about how I want my child to see me, what atmosphere I want to create," he says. "I want my child to have the freedom and opportunity to be what *he wants to be,* and not what I want him to be."

Carlos, concerned that his child might be adversely affected by his moodiness, wonders: "I want to help my child learn how to be the best person she can be. But if I'm having my own difficulties . . . how is she going to look at my failures—the times I'm not able to be the best *I* can be, when I fall down and make mistakes in judgment, or when I get angry? How's that going the affect her?"

Dominique has been focusing squarely on his relationship with his wife and their ability to parent together. "The more time we can spend with each other now," he says, "the better prepared we'll be for the initial shock of having our baby in our lives. It will take a special closeness to work out a way of having some freedom together and some freedom alone. I'm thinking about the actual demands on us—what our attitudes are going to be, how we'll act in different situations, and what we'll require of each other. We ought to have a consistent attitude right from the beginning. Are we going to pick up

Suzanne Arms

the baby each time we hear a cry or are we going to let the baby cry, or what?"

Health, Birth, and Other Worries. Feeling the baby move is a milestone event. It brings home the tangible reality of a growing fetus and an awareness that the course of gestation is beyond human control. From this moment on, you will be visited by intermittent concerns of one sort or another. You may at times wonder: Are "they" are getting enough rest, adequate exercise, sufficient relaxation, good nourishment? Complications such as long-term morning sickness, bleeding, or pain may intensify your worries, as may a previous miscarriage or a long-awaited conception. Although some degree of nervousness is understandable, concerns that persist and interfere with your enjoyment of pregnancy should be referred to your physician, midwife, or family therapist.

Nine months of pregnancy leaves much time for thinking, and for worrying. As the estimated date of arrival draws near, your focus will naturally turn toward the birth. A myriad of questions will arise: Will the labor be difficult? How can I be most helpful? Will I be helpful enough? What if I need to take a break? Will the birth practitioner arrive on time? Do I want to cut the cord? Will I be upset by the blood and by seeing my partner in pain? Will our baby be born healthy and vigorous? Your emotions will run the gamut from excitement and joy to uncertainty, nervousness, and impatience.

As soon as you think you are ready for the birth, you may become perplexed about how to parent a newborn. David frames his dilemma this way: "I'm not really sure how to act as a father. It's the kind of role that you don't know how to fill until it actually happens. You see and touch your baby, and suddenly, you're a father. I think it's an instinctual thing, like what a mother has with the baby. I think the father has a similar instinct. I'm just waiting for it all to be released." Indeed, when it comes to nagging concerns about parenting, we have no choice but to wait and see, and wish that time would move faster.

The worries that arise, bothersome as they can be, serve a constructive purpose: they signal a need for action *on our own behalf.* Whenever you notice an expanding bundle of concerns, stop and listen to them. What are they telling you? Do you perhaps need more

LET YOUR WORRIES BE YOUR GUIDE

To convert gnawing concerns into effective action, try one or more of the following activities:

- Check out educational videos about fetal development and childbirth. Read books about sexuality, relationship, parenting, and fathering.

- Watch childbirth movies, especially if you are nervous about witnessing the birth.

- Visit your physician or midwife, and bring along all your questions.

- Discuss your feelings, hopes, expectations, or needs with your partner.

- Talk with other fathers about *their* pregnancy and parenting experiences.

- Spend time with your parents. Ask them about your birth and infancy and what early parenthood was like for them.

- Create a special labor gift for your partner—something to keep beside her or on the wall while laboring and birthing.

- Create a welcome-to-the-world gift for your child.

- Begin thinking about who will do which jobs around the house after your baby is born.

information about this stage of your child's development, or about lovemaking? Do you need more time with your partner, friends, other parents, or your own parents? Would you like to do something special with your children or a close relative? Or maybe you'd like to pursue a personal interest, be with nature, get the nest ready and the house in order, or give up an unhealthy habit such as smoking.

Don't run from your worries. Let them steer you toward meaningful action.

Self-Confidence. Everything that happens during pregnancy will help you gain comfort and confidence in your evolution as a father-man. Key events can have special impact. Take note of them; you may even want to record them for posterity. Feeling his baby move has been profoundly meaningful for Alan. As he explains: "I can feel the baby clearly now and know when he is sleeping, kicking, or just moving around in there. The existence of my child is real at last. There's definitely someone there—someone I can identify with."

Even ordinary events—such as talking casually with other fathers, playing with children, or visiting your care provider—can be infused with new meaning. Bob, awaiting the arrival of his newborn, has spent many evenings baby-sitting with a friend's infant named Stephanie. Thrilled by her loving responses to him, Bob has begun "feeling like a father for the first time." He notes: "Thoughts are running through my head that shortly I am going to be dealing with a little person like Stephanie. It's really going to be intense, but I sure feel good thinking about it."

Pregnancy, thanks to nature's good planning, spans a long interval—precisely what is needed for taking stock of the unexpected, integrating the many subtle changes, and preparing for the reality of becoming a parent. Some men manage to adjust to their new identity by midpregnancy. Others remain uneasy until their children are born, or sometime afterward. Still others never overcome their discomfort and, regrettably, retreat from fatherhood altogether.

Confidence and security in paternity are rooted in *self-acceptance*, a precious commodity. Self-acceptance is the appreciation of who we are (rather than who we think we "should be"), a trait that is strengthened each time we stake a claim to our experiences (rather than ignoring them or wondering what we "should be" experiencing). In beginning to truly accept ourselves as we are, we uncover thoughts, feelings, dreams, and behaviors that were long ago silenced, and we recognize the shallowness and conditionality of the rules governing our lives. We discover, to our surprise and delight, that we are multidimensional and multifaceted: both strong and weak, generous and needy, serious and playful, mature and childlike. We see beyond old learned survival mechanisms and defenses—the games we played to secure acceptance and love.

Accepted and loved from *within*, we can set about reclaiming valuable aspects of ourselves. Growing into ourselves, we become centered, emotionally present, and more available to those we love.

Mary Motley Kalergis

Man struggles to find life outside himself, unaware that the life he's seeking is within him.

—Kahlil Gibran

CHAPTER 4

GETTING INVOLVED IN PREGNANCY

What can I do now that she's pregnant? Not much to say or do, really. I mean, I can't carry the baby for her. . . . It's her thing, I guess. I can just be around and wait it out. The good times will come later.

CHILDBEARING REMAINS A MYSTERY TO MEN, a wondrous, creative process that we can only imagine. Having no direct access to the sensations and biological events that so intimately connect child and mother, we perceive of our child as ever present, yet never present. Until we see or touch our newborn, he or she is always coming—never really here.

These realities become increasingly apparent as gestation progresses. The more we yearn to share intrinsically in the pregnancy and birth, the more disheartened we may be to find no apparent ways of fulfilling our longings.

The Wish to Be Included

Man's perennial struggle with his inability to carry, birth, and produce nourishment for his offspring has been recognized since time immemorial. Some early cultures wove dramatic stories and legends around this theme. Others devised elaborate male birthing rites, many of which are still in practice.

Creation Myths and Couvade Customs. The envy, inferiority, isolation, and insecurity men feel in the face of women's childbearing capacities are illustrated beautifully in creation mythologies from around the world. The Babylonian story of creation, for example, portrays the rebellion of the male gods against the Great Mother, Tiamat, who rules the universe. The tale opens with the male gods in counsel, deciding who will lead them in battle against her. Each contender must prove his ability to defeat the Great Mother by performing a daunting task: he must, through an act of will, destroy a ceremonial garment and then cause it to reappear. Marduk succeeds in this act of re-creation and is declared the supreme god. He eventually overpowers the Great Mother, slays her, and forms heaven and hell from her body.

Obsessed with establishing their superiority, these male gods see no alternative but to conquer the Great Mother. In doing so, they metaphorically destroy their connection to their own feminine nature—their receptive, nourishing, and creative capacities.

The Old Testament account of creation reverses the laws of nature. Here, woman does not give birth to man. Instead, God ("He") creates the world "by His Word"; later, Eve is born from Adam's rib. Greek mythology portrays a similar reversal. Zeus devours his pregnant wife, whereupon he gives birth to Athena and Dionysus.

Traditional cultures the world over—perhaps in recognition of the potent psychic forces unleashed in men on the verge of fatherhood—have developed practices that help expectant fathers deepen their identification with childbearing. These practices are collectively known as "couvade rituals." The word *couvade* is derived from the French *couver,* meaning "to incubate, hatch, or brood," and signifies the male's engagement with his unborn baby.

Some couvade rituals appear symbolic, entitling expectant fathers to certain privileges. During pregnancy, men are prohibited, from cutting, killing, eating particular foods, hunting, lifting heavy objects, or touching sharp utensils. As birth approaches, custom requires men to go into seclusion, or to imitate the sounds and movements of labor.[13]

Other couvade rituals involve fathers more directly in childbearing. The Arapesh father of New Guinea engages in frequent strenuous sexual activity to foster the healthy development of his unborn child. After the birth, he remains close to mother and child—so much so that he is commonly said to be "in bed having a baby."[14] The Sirionas father of Bolivia goes off to hunt when labor begins. His return is eagerly awaited, for only he is permitted to sever the umbilical cord. He later names his child after the first animal killed on his ceremonial hunt. The Zinacanteco father of Mexico tugs on a cinch around his laboring wife's waist to help expel their child. In several cultures, birthing women lean against their partners to help ease the baby's passage.[15]

Explanations of the couvade tradition vary widely. According to one, the rituals serve to trick evil spirits into pursuing an expectant father so that the mother and developing child may go unharmed. According to another, they awaken male nurturance.[16, 17] The rituals may *also* serve to underscore the male's importance in childbearing, or to protect mother and child from the envy or hostility an otherwise displaced father may be feeling.

Whatever their intent, couvade customs give expectant fathers in some parts of the world an opportunity to get close to the creative process and actively participate in the bearing and birthing of their newborns. Couvade rituals confirm an expectant father's special status when he may be feeling like a second-class citizen, and summon forth support from friends and relatives when he may be feeling confused, alienated, and alone.

Men without Myths and Rituals. We, in the United States, complain that fathers rarely see their adolescents, are emotionally detached from their school-age children, and are not motivated to establish bonds with their infants or young children. We are quick to stereotype these men as "deadbeat dads" and "Disneyland dads." Yet we have failed to provide our men with rites of passage or even a cultural context in which to express their yearnings to embrace a family life of their own creation.

Having no prototypes and no guidelines for being an involved expectant father can prove trying, if not exasperating. As Lenny sees it: "I go through periods where I'll be an ideal expectant father and be really involved and helpful, and then I'll go through another stage where I'll just want to get away from it all and not think about it. Sometimes I feel like I'm on a roller coaster."

Some men unconsciously form their own relationship to childbearing by developing sympathy symptoms—disturbances that seem to mimic those of the pregnant woman. The most commonly reported ailments include nausea, loss of appetite, weight gain, stomach bloating, and headaches. An estimated 15 to 50 percent of all expectant fathers manifest some sympathy symptoms. One child-birth educator found that expectant fathers in her classes gained an average of eighteen pounds—enough to facilitate the growth of a baby!

A variety of theories have been proposed to explain sympathy symptoms. The one I find most convincing depicts them as physical expressions of an emotional need to be *close to the sacred childbearing process*—to share in it, even if vicariously. Steve, an expectant father who gained more than ten pounds by his sixth month of pregnancy, is a case in point. "I don't know why I've gained all this weight," he states. "I know I've been eating more than usual, but there's something else. I never told this to anyone, but when I feel the roundness of my stomach, it's as though I've 'taken on' the pregnancy, even though I don't feel anything inside me. It's a funny thing, feeling pregnant together. I am more aware of us sharing the pregnancy, and that seems to open me up to feeling things more."

Although the true etiology of sympathy symptoms remains a matter of conjecture, it is interesting to note that fathers who exhib-

HOMING IN ON SYMPATHY SYMPTOMS

If you are experiencing physical symptoms during (or after) pregnancy, examine the message your body is sending you. Possible messages might be:

- I want to get closer to my partner.
- I want to get closer to my child.
- I want to nurture my child.
- I need _____.
- I'm upset or nervous about _____.
- I feel left out. I'd like more attention.

it them, compared with those who do not, feel significantly more positive about their pregnancies. In the postpartum period, these men also assume more child care tasks.

Facing the Losses

Paradoxically, the man about to gain a son or daughter may concurrently sense a strong undercurrent of loss. In addition to feeling left out and unable to involve himself to any meaningful degree in the pregnancy, he misses the exclusivity of his prepregnancy relationship with his partner. Moreover, any attempts on his part to reestablish intimacy are likely to be less than satisfying, for the psychophysiology of gestation has a commanding rhythm and timetable of its own.

Jealousy, Insecurity, Frustration. Expectant fathers walk a fine line. They are called upon to juggle their own magnified emotional needs with their desire to be responsive partners. Complicating things further, scores of well-meaning books about pregnancy as well as thousands of professionals—unaware that fathers must work to stay in touch with an emotional process of their own—rank attentiveness to the pregnant woman's needs as the measure of their effectiveness as partners.

Acts of genuine caring and attentiveness—gifts of love freely offered—generate joy. Acts performed in obligatory fulfillment of some role expectation do not. Indeed, countless couples who play out their prescribed roles to perfection awaken years later to find themselves engaged in an unsatisfying *arrangement* rather than a loving relationship. What the advice-givers fail to convey is that attention bestowed on a loved one at the expense of self-caring spells trouble. *Interest, empathy, and nurturing will flow spontaneously when a man is in touch with his own vitality.*

The expectant father who feels both displaced and frustrated in his efforts to recapture a sense of closeness with his partner is susceptible to a number of overt or covert emotional states. Joseph, well aware of his reaction, remarks: "I feel jealous, afraid that I'm going to be shut out. I'm feeling very left out now and concerned that I'll be excluded from the strong mother-child relationship. My wife is pregnant; it's her thing. I'm kind of a bystander."

Raul is in a different quandary. Early in pregnancy, he perceived "dramatic changes" in his wife. Kate had suddenly become sullen and withdrawn, demanding more time and attention. At first, Raul responded by "trying to keep pace with her demands," spending more time at home and making love pretty much on demand "to let her know I loved her and still found her attractive." Now, about a month later, he is feeling "cradled in." He is eager to "take back" some of his "space"—a realization that is causing him great consternation because Kate's needs "seem so pressing."

The problem, as Raul is to discover, is not that his partner's needs are so insistent but that they are *overshadowing his own*. In his view: "It's like she's moving so fast through it. I'm into my work. I'll come home, and right away I'm supposed to get into the whole expectancy thing with her. There are times when I just can't do it— can't make that transition. Sometimes I need time to relax, to be alone. . . . I feel like going to sleep or running off somewhere. It's like normally having a certain amount of freedom, and then suddenly having it taken away."

Jealousy, insecurity, and frustration, no matter how fleeting, are difficult for many men to acknowledge and accept. We have been taught that displays of jealousy (especially toward our partner and child) and insecurity expose us as weak, unmasculine. Frustration is to be handled, controlled ("No problem, man"), or managed lest it turn to anger or resentment, in which case we may be seen as "not having it all together," or worse, "losing it." In adhering to these precepts, what a Gordian knot we tie ourselves into!

If you find yourself in one of these states, try not to be alarmed. Regard it as a natural response to the multitude of changes ushered in by pregnancy. For a better understanding of your predicament, try stepping back to look at the bigger picture.

Inside the Pregnant Mother. Early in pregnancy, the expectant mother turns inward, becoming self-absorbed and, in all likelihood, less accessible. She, too, is apt to be unprepared, apprehensive, and uncertain of her new role. Striving to shape her mothering identity, she may be thinking about her relationship with *her* mother. Or she may be absorbed in the physiological changes taking place within her, or in fantasies about the unknown child she is carrying. She may be embarrassed, ambivalent, resentful, or frightened. Whatever your partner's experiences may be, the idea of discussing them with you may seem a colossal expenditure of energy. Besides, she may assume that you are not particularly interested in her pregnancy problems. (Does this sound familiar?)

As the growing fetus makes its presence known, your partner may become further preoccupied, intrigued by the mysterious being growing inside her. By mid- to late pregnancy, reassured that her child is developing properly and indeed has a life independent of hers, she may feel relieved—perhaps for the first time in months. Less self-absorbed, she is apt to become more protective of the unborn baby.

The later months of pregnancy bring extra weight, a shift in balance, and physical discomforts that can interfere with daily routines. Her time with you may become markedly curtailed. She may no longer have the energy for sunset hikes and may be too uncomfortable to make love, or even sit through a movie.

If your partner seems to be screening you out at any point during pregnancy, try to understand that rather than rejecting you, she is most likely preoccupied. This awareness, although perhaps not very consoling, can help you come to terms with the loss you are facing.

Defenses Up and Working. If you have been feeling especially frustrated, unimportant, or abandoned, the thought of decamping may have crossed your mind. Many expectant fathers do leave the "camp," investing themselves in work, hobbies, and relationships outside the family. Taking more time for yourself can, when pursued with clear intentions, renew your enthusiasm, perspective, and sense of purpose. It did for Lou, who says: "I have noticed this need to create. I'm growing a vegetable garden, and I've put a lot of energy into that. It's really important to me—the idea of producing something myself. I've also written a paper. I've been wanting to *bring something about*. That's really a very fundamental force in my life now, whereas usually it isn't."

Exercise caution, however, because leave-taking can become a habitual escape—a flight from hurt feelings, frustrated needs, discomforts, and fears. Fleeing is an inborn protective response to a physically threatening situation. Running from uncomfortable situations is another matter entirely, and one with potentially serious consequences. Relationships do break up during and after pregnancy. Extramarital affairs and spousal abuse reach statistically significant levels during this period as well.

If you are staying away for long periods of time, or thinking of doing so, assess the circumstances: Why is your impulse to leave so strong? Are you feeling threatened? If so, by what? What might happen if you decide to stay? More than likely, the fears stalking you are the beasts commonly aroused during the transition to parenthood. To disempower them, give them names: *unfamiliarity, uncertainty, lack of control, anxiety, loneliness,* or whatever seems most relevant. If you persist in avoiding contact with your partner, turning inward and silent, or outward for attention, ask yourself why. *Which feelings or needs are you trying to escape from?*

One new father who considered leaving during pregnancy, offers this counsel: "I think it's really important for a woman to help her husband feel at ease and realize he's wanted, during pregnancy especially. A man has a tendency to get kind of lost in the shuffle, and not be as important a person as he was before. . . . I think I needed more than I got. If I had been more vocal, my wife would surely have been more understanding toward me. But I kind of held it inside. That was a big mistake."

Old Wounds. When responses to loss are powerful and unrelenting, they can be rooted in memories of unhealed emotional injuries sustained in childhood. On the path to fatherhood this may be especially true, for dotting the trails are periodic reminders of childhood pain—the neglect, criticism, invalidation, and lack of love we felt, especially from the fathers we looked to for love and wanted to please.

If your sense of loss hurls you backward, take heart. Out of the desire to heal past wounds arises the inspiration to become the parents we always wanted. Fatherhood presents us with rich opportunities for healing and growing beyond our wildest expectations. As lecturer and author Paul Brenner, MD, muses, "Maybe the drive that motivates us to bear a child is our longing to rekindle that lost innocence or incompleteness of our own childhood and allow us a second chance to create ourselves anew."[18]

When Loss Turns to Abuse. Too often, a man's response to the loss of his prepregnant relationship remains unmitigated. Prompted by a long history of deprivation and neglect, he may lash out in anger or numb his pain with drugs or alcohol, further undermining his efforts to solidify the relationship and his potential for personal growth. Without professional help, he is likely to become, in time, a wounded father. And his child, like those of all wounded fathers, will carry the pain of a father's unexplored life.

Bombarded daily with heart-wrenching accounts of trauma resulting from father absence or neglect, substance abuse, incest, and physical or emotional battering, we are being infiltrated by an enemy of our own creation: *rampant violence.* Clearly, involved fatherhood must become a national priority. Ensuring the male presence in labor and childbirth, although a giant step in the right direction, falls far short of securing the father an intimate place in his child's life. For that, legislation is needed. Policies and initiatives must be drafted to encourage father involvement in *every* aspect of family care.

Ultimately, fathers *themselves* must take responsibility for healing their wounds and creating a healthy, nonviolent world. Positive intent will not suffice, for we cannot change what we are unaware of, we cannot foster in others what we do not allow in ourselves, and we cannot nurture another's growth until we have breathed life into our own. For a man to willingly wrap himself in the cloak of fatherhood, he must first go inward and begin to love himself.

Healing Ourselves

Men often speak of pain in curious ways: "Oh, it's nothing . . . didn't hurt a bit" or "It'll blow over." After it has blown over, and back again, we tell ourselves: "The past is the past. Leave it alone and move into the present." Accustomed to pushing aside past discomforts and fears, we tend to feel *doubly* jeopardized during the countdown to labor and birth. We do not want to disembark; nor do we want to wallow aimlessly in past injustices. And we certainly do not want to create a life of misery for our child.

What can a father-in-waiting do about old hurts? He can "watch" them, "listen to" them, and acknowledge them. When you *allow* yourself to touch and accept all that you are experiencing, without trying to "make" anything happen, you discover that change takes place by itself—free of planning, free of struggling to "make" it happen.

Harbinger of Hope. At some point when you least expect anything to occur, a visitor will enter your field of awareness, look you in the eye hard and strong, then whisper in your ear: "It's time to decide. No slipping away now. *Are you willing to prepare for fatherhood?* Are you willing to do it *today?*"

You already know that willingness of this sort entails opening to the unfamiliar, facing whatever comes your way, wrestling with fears, making mistakes, being vulnerable, and being real. What will be your reply?

Fully aware that no one can make this decision for you and that to not respond is to respond, you may wish to ask the visitor a few questions of your own, such as: Why should I set out on this difficult adventure? What's in this journey for *me?* What will involved fatherhood *do* for me? The answer is, as increasing numbers of men are discovering: More than you can possibly imagine.

Fathering Truths. The most marvelous untold truth is that involved fatherhood *makes* the man. Fatherhood is very often a man's most satisfying life activity. Sam Keen drives this point home when he writes, "A man who takes no care of and is not involved in the process of caring for and initiating the young remains a boy no matter what his achievements."[19] The Pueblo Indians of the American Southwest offer this wisdom: "He who knows not the love of a small child cannot know the love of the Great Spirit."[20]

Rewards awaiting the fatherman include innumerable opportunities for:

- Overcoming isolation and detachment.
- Finding meaning, pride, and an immeasurable sense of accomplishment.
- Heightening compassion, trust, tolerance, patience, unselfishness, passion, and unconditional love.
- Enhancing self-esteem and creativity.
- Establishing linkage to the world of our forefathers and the larger family of fathers.

Anna Propp Covici

- Healing childhood pain. Many men report that the pain carried from a childhood tarnished by mistreatment eases dramatically as they begin taking care of their own children.

Ritualizing Your Pregnancy. To ritualize is to make sacred that which is ordinary. To ritualize your pregnancy is to celebrate with reverence your participation in bringing forth new life. If your family or community has not passed on personally meaningful pregnancy customs, consider creating one for yourself. Any format will do, as long as it helps you participate in fatherhood openly, authentically, and as early as possible.

Until a clear design for your ritual takes shape, the old mainstays may be suitable. In addition to visiting the doctor or midwife, plan a joint baby shower with your partner, and invite close friends. Shop together for baby furniture, clothing, and soft toys. Envision yourself catching your newborn, cutting the umbilical cord, holding your baby close, singing your favorite songs, calling your friends, bathing and massaging your newborn—in other words, prepare now to bond with your partner and newborn *right there in the birthing room.*

Also brew up some partnership rituals. Watch videos together about different birthing options such as hospital births, homebirths, birth center births, water births, and squatting births; discuss books about birthing and parenting (see pages 181–184); share dreams, memories, hopes, and fantasies; begin thinking together about the naming of your baby; keep pregnancy journals; bathe together by candlelight; give each other ceremonial foot rubs; meditate together; get out the camera and take "belly" movies; play music and compose songs, poems, and limericks for your baby. Allow these activities to bring out the learner in you, the lover in you, the child in you, and the father in you. Try not to be inhibited. If it feels good, do it!

Ritualizing your pregnancy together will add a new dimension to your relationship. It will help you see the higher purpose of your union and honor it as a living entity apart from your individual concerns. Ask yourselves: What does this baby mean in our lives? Are we continuing a family pattern? Are we shifting generational patterns? How will our relationship contribute to the future?

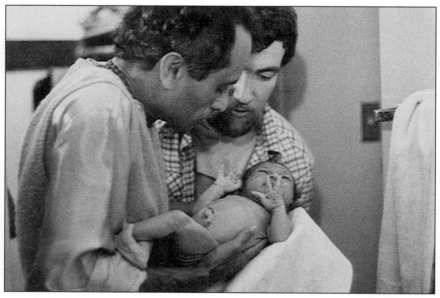

Sszanne Arms

BONDING WITH YOUR MYSTERY BABY

To bond with your baby in utero, and at the same time draw closer to your partner, all that is required is willingness and a little imagination. Here are some suggestions:

- Read about gestational growth or watch educational videos about prenatal development. Getting to know what is happening in your child's life from week to week will help "bring the pregnancy home."
- Learn about the relationship between nutrition and fetal development. Be proud of the knowledge you acquire. Consult with your partner about the best nutrients for your developing child.
- Investigate childbirth classes, birthing options, physician or midwife protocols, hospital policies, and infant massage techniques.
- Listen to your child's heartbeat. Feel the kicks; notice the hiccups. Talk and croon to your child, and be on the lookout for responses to your loving sounds.
- Prepare the nest. Fix what's broken; buy or create what's needed; and build something new, just for your baby.
- Give to yourself. Take time to be with yourself; nourish yourself. Meditating and walking outdoors can help you recover your inner rhythm and tune in to the gestation and birthing in the world of nature.
- Find a time and place to be "alone" with your child (perhaps while cuddling quietly with your partner or after she has fallen asleep). Making contact through your wife's belly, allow yourself to relax, then touch, kiss, or converse with your unborn child. Direct positive thoughts and loving feelings to your infant. If you wish, visualize yourself holding, touching, rocking, or talking and singing to your child. Then let this image and the sensations connecting you to your child become etched into your consciousness. Relive this experience each day.

Be sure to reach into the community as well. Talking with other fathers, holding newborns, and playing with infants and young children will remind you of the father love you already have.

Ritualizing your pregnancy may be the most powerful way there is to "take in" the sacred events that are unfolding in the world of your developing child. Pregnancy rituals serve as initiation and reclamation, setting you smack dab in the middle of nature's grand design.

Michael Weisbrot

A child, like any creation or work of art, changes all that precedes it.

—Paul Brenner

CHAPTER 5

AS RELATIONSHIPS CHANGE

Being a father is different from not being a father. And somehow that makes me a different person. Now, as an expectant father, I'm treated differently too. It's hard to describe just how. It's very subtle. Others are ascribing new characteristics to me all the time. And this changes the way I identify with people I see in the world.

THE WAYS IN WHICH PEOPLE RESPOND to an expectant father can have a pronounced influence on how he sees himself and adjusts to his new role.

Suddenly, old relationships take on new meaning. Friends, relatives, colleagues, coworkers, classmates, neighbors, even the mail carrier become catalysts for growth. Their words serve as a mirror in which the expectant father recognizes and affirms his new identity. Their perceptions help ground him in the task ahead.

People often regard an expectant father in a fresh light. At the same time, *he* is looking at *them* through new eyes.

Old Friends, New Friends

I recall announcing my first pregnancy to friends. I had just begun graduate studies, and my wife had temporarily given up her job. Most of our friends were married and stepping into careers; none were pregnant. Although nearly all our friends had thought about having children and some had planned on parenting in the future, none were planning to start a family in the *near* future.

The announcement of our pregnancy stirred things up. Women

friends reacted in a variety of ways. Those in their late twenties and early thirties seemed to suddenly begin counting the ticks on the biological clock and reassessing their goals. Others started looking critically at the quality of their marriages. Several of my wife's friends withdrew from her, remaining curious from afar, watching and wondering what effect pregnancy might have on *them.*

My wife and I talked often about the rejection and alienation she was feeling with her friends retreating "as if pregnancy were a communicable disease." Able to view the situation a bit more objectively, I reassured her: "Your friends just aren't ready to face *their* issues about pregnancy. Let's not take it personally. I'm with you. Becoming parents is good for us. And that's what really counts, isn't it?"

Following our daughter's birth, many of my wife's friends regrouped around her and began spending time with her and Becky. Apparently satisfied that everything had turned out OK, their curiosity had drawn them closer.

Feelings of social isolation are common during pregnancy. Friends, especially those unable to relate to childbearing, often fade into the background. To overcome their sense of aloneness, many pregnant couples begin seeking out new friendships and developing an expanding circle of friends with interests and values more similar to their own.

New friendships were not what Joel and Carol had in mind. Upon hearing news of the pregnancy, many of Joel's friends seemed "cold and judgmental," which left him feeling confused and defensive. Despite his strong desire to have a family, he began worrying about being "tied down" with a newborn. As the pregnancy progressed, he began feeling "somehow older" than his friends, more removed from them than he had anticipated. In time, Joel and Carol began gravitating toward friendships with other expectant couples and some new parents.

"The goals we've set," Joel explained some weeks later, "lie very much between those of one group of friends who want to head out to farm the land or build a boat to carry them around the world and those of the other group who are fashioning their lives around children, a home, a lawn, and a dog. Straddling these two lifestyles is a very difficult thing. We wonder if we'll be able to do what we want once there's a child in our lives. Still, we realize that we want a child very much."

Joel and Carol's new parenting friendships provided a "home base" to return to while exploring their evolving concerns. The contact was particularly gratifying to Joel, who surprised himself by forming "an immediate common bond" with these new friends and "falling into the parent's role easily while around them."

Another couple, Eric and Ann, were living together upon learning of their pregnancy. One of Eric's immediate concerns was how his new status would affect his relationships with single friends. He discussed his doubts with Ann, all the while maintaining frequent contact with his longtime friends. In time, Eric developed close relationships with several fathers. These new contacts helped him "feel like a father." He explains: "I had always related to parenthood as the viewer or outsider. Children were always somebody else's kids. I had plenty of opinions about the right way to approach different situations—the right way to handle this or that. Anyway, as I was speaking with Paul, another father, a kind of identification seeped into me. It suddenly became real. I felt a strong sense of myself as a father. It is a little strange to realize that I am *already* a father— even though the baby's not here yet."

You, too, may wake up one day to discover a broadening circle of friends, many of whom are themselves adjusting to pregnancy and parenthood. If you do, welcome them in. These people can help you realign your priorities and serve as invaluable sources of information, support, and contact. As one expectant father puts it: "You often wonder how your life's going to work out with a child in it. I'm so relieved to know that people I respect are having success at being parents. Gaining contact with parents of babies has stimulated a significant change and, almost right away, the sense of a common bond."

The Parent-to-Parent Challenge

The inevitability of parenthood will simultaneously thrust you into the future and hurl you into the past. Advancing and retreating through time serves an important psychological purpose. Reviewing your childhood, understanding your development, and tackling unfinished business with family members will help prepare you to step into an active fathering role.

Your relationship with your parents may already be shifting. While looking to them for support and guidance you may also be stepping away, examining your childhood, their relationship with each other, and their individual strengths and shortcomings. *Pregnancy suddenly places you face-to-face with your mother and father on the common ground of parenthood.* As one expectant mother comments, "Now they're people, not just parents."

In time, you will discover an emerging sense of your new family as an entity distinct from your family of origin. In the words of an eight-month-pregnant father: "I'm already feeling a pretty complete identification with my own family—apart from the family I grew up with. It feels more like a family than anything ever did before. It's a separate unit, different from my wife's family, too, and every other family in the world. And yet, I'm carrying on my family name, which feels good as well."

Ellen Eichler

Your father-to-father relationship is certainly subject to change. The transit from being a son to being a father can be awesome, challenging, and inspiring, particularly for a man accustomed to a large gap in experience between himself and his father. Many newly expectant fathers speak of a growing desire to get to know their fathers. Others, tapping in to old resentments, become critical of their fathers, especially for their long absences, insensitivities, and apparent lack of caring. Recollections of good times surface as well. By the end of pregnancy, a man is likely to be on new terms with his father and more forgiving of his mistakes.

Your father-to-mother relationship will also change. An expectant father gives considerable thought to the woman who gave birth to him and to the mothering he received. A man may be suddenly flooded with memories of his mother's loving or not-so-loving ways. Or he may recall the impressions he had while watching his father mistreat his mother, or vice versa. He may wonder what his own birth was like, what his mother was feeling at the time, and how his presence affected his parents' relationship. By the final months of pregnancy, a man may well have acquired a new appreciation for his mother and, by extension, his pregnant partner.

Expectant Grandparents

Prospective grandparents can be an invaluable resource during and following pregnancy. Shared stories about their parenting experiences—the joys, doubts, and resolutions—along with their offerings of sensitivity, perspective, and support can be especially satisfying to couples who need approval and validation of their new parenting status.

Hearing about events that lie beyond the reach of your memory will add a rich dimension to your journey. Talking about the good and bad times, the happy and sad times, will enlarge the scope of your exchange with your parents. An honest sharing of *your* childhood recollections can also help heal the rifts that may still exist in your relationship with your parents. Moreover, looking at family patterns can help you and your partner avoid slipping into unwanted parenting, relationship, birthing, or feeding styles.

Anna Propp Covici

According to several birth practitioners, a woman who remains uninformed about her mother's labor patterns, for example, can inadvertently repeat them—right down to an unwarranted cesarean section. So test the grandparenting waters, proceed carefully, yet *do* proceed. You'll be delighted at what you find.

A Grandparent's Transition. Becoming a grandparent for the first time, a transition in its own right, often gives rise to conflicting emotions. The promise of a new generation may evoke in your parents deep satisfaction and renewed hope that the family will move beyond hitherto unrealized dreams and expectations. Yet, having gained an about-to-be-born grandchild, your parents may also be struggling with the loss of a child, for you will never need them in the same ways as before. In effect, they may be simultaneously mourning and rejoicing.

The majority of new grandparents eventually work out their ambivalent feelings. Spending time with their grandchild, discovering the rewards of grandparenthood—their grandchild's fascination and love and your appreciation for their contributions—your parents will too. In the meantime, try to be understanding of the emotional tasks they are grappling with, and avoid taking their ambivalence personally.

Expectant grandparents who are facing life crises or are distressed about aging do not adjust as quickly and easily as others. Those who are unhappy with their lives can become more dependent on their children or intrusively involved in their lives, posing an added obstacle.

This was true for Jay. An only son, Jay was "his father's boy." Father and son had maintained unusually close ties throughout Jay's college years. Their relationship began to change, however, when Jay married and moved out of state. Although he could sense that he and his father were drifting apart, he could not imagine what he had done to effect this change. Four years later, in the middle of his pregnancy, he began having recurrent dreams about his father.

Jay described one dream as follows: "I am swimming in a lake and am starting to feel very tired. I'm waving to a nearby boat. The man aboard looks like my father; it *is* him! I'm relieved. My dad looks at me, but ignores my calls for help. I can't believe it—he keeps circling around me! Why? What is he doing? I'm desperate now, calling, 'Hey Dad, help me out of here. I'm exhausted. Get me out of here!' He hears me, but keeps going around. What's happening here? Why is he doing this to me? 'Dad, come here. Bring over the boat, damn it!'" The dream ends with his dad finally, but reluctantly, letting Jay aboard. They row to shore without speaking a word.

While discussing this dream, Jay explained that each time he had reached out for contact, support, or guidance during pregnancy, he had felt his father's hesitancy and evasiveness. Jay went on to acknowledge his hurt and disappointment when his father "removed himself" emotionally after Jay's marriage. Now Jay was hurt again because his father—who "knew the waters"—remained unenthusiastic and unavailable.

I encouraged Jay to return to the dream and engage his father in a conversation. Imagining his father's words, Jay began to understand how difficult it was for his father to let go of him: unfulfilled in his other relationships, Jay's father could see only that he was losing a son, not that he was gaining a daughter-in-law and subsequently a grandchild. Jay also discovered that he had been feeling guilty for moving away from his parents, with no intent of returning to raise his child.

Able to view the larger picture, Jay began to understand his resentment toward his father. He decided then and there to stop shouldering guilt over his decision to leave his old neighborhood. Releasing himself from the burden of blame enabled Jay to rekindle his appreciation for his father and to reestablish a healthy relationship with him.

Across the Generations. If you and your parents, or your partner and hers, are getting stuck in murky waters, try to remember that you are *all* going through major transitions. The following tips can help ease the passage for everyone:

- Meet with prospective grandparents to talk about your current needs. Also discuss how and when grandparental assistance will be most helpful in the postpartum weeks. Ask about *their* needs and expectations too.
- Avoid hosting more than one set of grandparents at the same time. To keep the scales balanced, alternate visits.
- *Grandparents:* Temper your advice with wisdom, moderation, and sensitivity. Realize that your adult child—as well as each member of the growing family—is wrestling with rapid change and difficult adjustments. Recall what these months were like for you. Review the communication exercises in chapter 8, and strive for a smoother transition for yourselves and your children. Also encourage and support the expectant father's involvement with his child; give instructions sparingly and thoughtfully.

Dave Rusk

Sex may teach a man and woman the delight of coming together; marriage may suffuse us with the comfort and healing that comes from knowing and being known; but it takes a child to tutor us in the virtue of hope.

—Sam Keen

CHAPTER 6

SEX AND THE PREGNANT COUPLE

Is it really all right to be sexually active during pregnancy?
For how long? What about orgasms? Is it normal to feel very
sexual sometimes and completely turned off at other times?

SEXUAL LIBERATION HAS HARDLY MADE A DENT in our understanding of
sexuality during pregnancy. Misperceptions abound. Clear, accurate
literature on the subject is hard to come by, and many perinatal professionals are either too busy or unwilling to discuss such "personal" matters in any depth.

Consequently some expectant couples, concerned about the
safety of lovemaking during pregnancy, fall prey to age-old presumptions about what should and should not be done. For others,
talking about sexual feelings, needs, and preferences—an activity
difficult at *any* time—comes to an abrupt halt. Being turned on and
passionate becomes suddenly taboo.

Although sexual routines often do fluctuate during pregnancy,
they should not be eliminated altogether. Indeed, during pregnancy, a
couple's sexual relationship can become *more enjoyable and satisfying*
than before. What is needed is patience, understanding, a desire to
address sexual feelings and fears, and a willingness to experiment with
new ways of pleasuring each other.

Through the Trimesters

The fires of love burn capriciously over the thirty-five or so weeks
of pregnancy. Each trimester seems to bring a metamorphosis of
its own.

The First Trimester. While adjusting to her newly pregnant state, your partner may be wrestling with morning sickness (not necessarily limited to the morning hours), increased tenderness in her breasts, mood swings, fatigue, and irritability. Self-conscious about her appearance, she may lose touch with her sensuality, and her interest in intercourse may wane.

During these three months, you may start missing the familiarity of the partnership you once knew. Or you may be fearful of losing your partner's love. If your normal avenues of expressing affection are impeded and your sexual advances rejected, you may begin detaching from the relationship. As David says in his second month of pregnancy: "Since the minute of confirmation, everything has changed dramatically. Her whole personality changed totally, and our relationship did also. It's been very sudden and drastic. I mean, I can see the hormones working! I feel like an *outsider* to all this."

If the early period of pregnancy seems to wash over your conjugal bliss like a tidal wave, try not to panic. Factors beyond your control and your partner's have been at work. The good news is that this state of affairs is not destined to continue. The tidewaters will soon recede, whereupon your partner will regain her energy and her interest in lovemaking.

The Second Trimester. Many pregnant women approach the second trimester with a heightened desire for sexual contact. Why the turnabout? Because as the physiological discomforts of the first three months subside, the expectant mother starts easing into her body and settling into her pregnancy. She may regard her new shape and newly kicking baby as affirmations of her femininity. Then, too, elevated levels of the sex hormones progesterone and estrogen are surging through her bloodstream.

How does a man approach the second trimester? More often than not, with a *diminished* sex drive. His decreased interest in sex may spring from concern about his partner's comfort or preoccupation with the responsibilities of fatherhood. Fearful of rejection and hoping to head off disappointment, he may be reluctant to engage in sexual encounters altogether.

This diminished male sex drive coincides with changes in the pregnant woman's body—her new shape, scent, and feel. A man may decide that there is "no room" for him, or "too much room." The baby's movement during lovemaking can be equally disturbing. Some men feel intruded upon, as if "someone" were "watching." Others believe *they* are intruding on the *baby*. In reality, fetal movement is simply a reflexive response to sound or motion. The baby is neither meddling in the lovemaking nor distressed by it.

Additional forces contributing to the decreased sex drive include a history of miscarriage, premature labor, placenta previa, and other pregnancy complications. Men who have accompanied their partners through such difficulties sometimes fear that penetration will hurt the baby or interfere with the pregnancy. Concerns of this sort, while understandable, are *not* substantiated by research. Although vigorous lovemaking during pregnancy may at times cause a small amount of bleeding from the newly softened and engorged blood vessels within the cervix, healing is usually rapid. Bleeding of this sort can be prevented by using positions that discourage deep penetration, as described later in this chapter. (Cervicitis, or inflammation of the cervix, can also cause spotting after intercourse, and may be treated medically.) Prenatal care providers generally encourage couples with no history of miscarriage and no signs of spotting to relax and enjoy lovemaking.

Religious and quasi-scientific claims can play a more subtle role in the second-trimester downshifting of sexuality. You may hear, for example, that frequent intercourse and female orgasm deprive the fetus of oxygen, or that intercourse with a pregnant woman is unsanitary and unnatural. Neither of these assertions is worth a moment of reflection.

The Third Trimester. Many women become less sexually active during the last three months of pregnancy. Some limit their lovemaking because they think they are supposed to or because they assume their partner is not interested. Others refrain out of fear of infecting the fetus or of initiating premature labor through orgasm. A large number of women are constrained by physical discomforts and reduced mobility. None of these factors, however, need get in the way of a richly sexual grand finale to pregnancy.

What are the medical parameters of third-trimester intercourse? Physicians routinely call a halt to lovemaking two to four weeks

KEEPING LOVE ALIVE

Whether or not your interest in lovemaking has dwindled, take time to ask yourself a few questions:

- How do you feel making love to your pregnant partner—uneasy, cautious, restrained, turned on?
- While looking at her enlarged abdomen and breasts, how do you feel—neutral, turned on, turned off, left out?
- How do you feel about your sexual relationship right now—confused, apprehensive, rejected, resentful, satisfied, exhilarated?

Are your sentiments less than rousing? If so, why? What will you do to recapture your vibrancy and ardor?

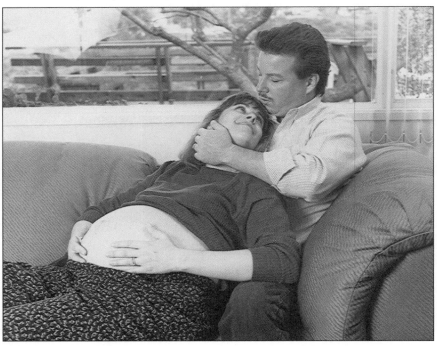

Miguel Pisarro

before a woman's estimated due date. This is an arbitrary yardstick and is rarely tailored to a couple's unique pregnancy conditions. Early cessation of intercourse is justified if there is bleeding or a risk of prematurity, or if the membranes have ruptured. In the absence of these conditions, restrictions on lovemaking not only are unjustified, but can impede the important bonding that takes place prior to the birth of a child.

What is the likelihood of transmitting infection to the fetus through intercourse? Research indicates that penetration in late pregnancy will not pose a problem before the membranes have ruptured. Besides, healthy couples are no more likely to develop an infection during pregnancy than they are at other times.[21]

As for orgasm, there is no need to worry. In uncomplicated pregnancies, orgasm *before term* does not trigger labor. Orgasm *at term*, when the cycle of pregnancy is complete, can occasionally kick off labor—activating contractions far more manageable than those set off by castor oil, pitocin, or other common labor inducers. In fact, lovemaking at term has many proven benefits and goes a long way toward preparing the mother for birth. Sucking on her nipples and genital stimulation can activate slow contractions. Prostaglandin, a component of semen, can naturally soften her cervix, paving the way to an easier labor. The elevations in maternal heart rate that sometimes accompany orgasm have no adverse effect on the fetus. Nor has any correlation been found between incidence of orgasm and prematurity.[22]

Similarly, third-trimester aches, pains, and lack of agility need not put a damper on lovemaking. Positional adjustments and inventive approaches are easy to incorporate into any sexual repertoire.

Alternative Lovemaking

Partners who pleasure each other during the months of gestation bond deeply before birth. To sustain lovemaking throughout your pregnancy, be creative. Together, you can find a variety of ways to accommodate your partner's changing shape and shifting center of balance. Here are some options that have proven satisfying to many pregnant couples.

Female-above-Male Position. Performed on a firm surface, this is an ideal position for early and midpregnancy. Your partner straddles you, either by squatting with her weight on her feet or by balancing on her knees, whichever is most comfortable.

Side-by-Side Position. Your partner lies on her side, then you align your body with hers, heart to heart.

Male-Facing-Seated-Female Position. This arrangement is perfect for the latter stages of pregnancy, when your partner's abdomen is significantly enlarged. She braces her weight on the front edge of a straight-backed chair and leans backward to rest her upper back against the back of the chair. You kneel, perhaps on a pad or pillow, directly in front of her between her open thighs. This position facilitates kissing, breast stimulation, and lots of face-to-face contact.

Rear-Entry Position. Your partner stands, resting her chest or elbows on a chair or counter—or she may prefer to kneel, resting her chest or elbows on a chair seat, stool, or stack of pillows. You approach her from behind, either straddling her buttocks or with your legs between hers, whichever is most comfortable.

Noncoital Sexual Activity. There are dozens of ways to express sensuality and eroticism—among them, oral-genital sex (fellatio and cunnilingus), nongenital fondling, mutual masturbation, bathing, sexually intimate conversation, and sharing erotic memories and sexual fantasies. Try facial massage, perineal massage (an episiotomy preventative), foot rubs, and thigh, belly, breast, and buttocks massages with vitamin E-rich oils to keep your partner's stretching skin elastic. Take turns massaging each other.

Lovemaking without intercourse can be especially meaningful for women victims of incest or rape, who may have developed an aversion to sex during pregnancy. And it can be a tender gift of love to a woman recovering from an invasive obstetric procedure or birth itself.

Accommodating the need for variety in your lovemaking may at first feel awkward or anxiety provoking. To set yourself at ease, think of each endeavor as a ready-made opportunity to explore new ways of pleasuring each other and adding excitement to your relationship. Above all, take things slowly. If you or your partner are not enjoying a new position or activity, go back to one you are comfortable with; then after a while, if you like, try something else. Impromptu sensuality is one of life's most bounteous feasts.

Sex and Loving

Concentrating on the frequency of lovemaking can raise anxiety levels. To avoid getting inadvertently caught up in the mathematics of intercourse, focus on other expressions of reassurance, closeness, gentleness, and emotional release. Remember that the frequency of sexual intercourse is far less important than the quality of your contact and communication with each other.

Alan and Karen had been sexually active until their eighth month of pregnancy. Now, with two months to go, they are, in Alan's words, "less sexual, more just being at home together, sitting, talking, and planning." Reflecting on this abrupt change in their sexual patterns, he explains: "It's almost like we're two old people sitting around together. Kind of a neat platonic relationship. Sex is not an important part of what's going on right now. I'm finding that not having to think of the sexual aspect of our relationship kind of opens up a whole different avenue—other important parts of our relationship are being exposed."

Adjusting to decreased lovemaking did not come as easily to Robert and Natalie. Robert confided: "When we found out Natalie was pregnant, we were afraid to do *any*thing! We didn't know what we *could* do and what the limits were. We were sort of taking it easy. This was a really big change in our sexual behavior. . . . After we got over the initial impact of her being pregnant, we were going a little bit further each time, in terms of how actively and hard we would make love. It was less satisfying for me and for her. That kind of peaked, then slipped down to where we made love maybe once every couple of weeks because right at orgasm, she would let out a scream or something would go wrong. We just didn't know what moves were OK. We haven't been able to figure that out because she's changing so quickly."

Now, nearing the end of their pregnancy, Robert and Natalie have decided to try new sexual positions. Despite months of resistance, they are thrilled with the results.

As you and your partner modify your loving ways, keep all lines of communication open. Talking about your changing sexuality can lead to gratifying resolutions and enhanced contact. Your partner needs to know, above all, that you find her attractive and desirable; if you keep silent on this or other important matters, she may assume that you do not find her appealing and are no longer interested in the pregnancy. The repercussions of such gross misunderstandings often carry over into the postpartum period, when intimacy and sexual harmonizing become even more challenging. So take time to communicate your interests, and do your part in staving off misperceptions.

The notion that sexuality wanes as pregnancy progresses is a myth that must be dispelled. Many women feel more sexually vibrant and feminine during pregnancy than ever before. By the same token, many men find their pregnant wives exceedingly attractive. As Steve recalls: "Having my wife pregnant around me so much, I was able to appreciate just how *beautiful* she was. Pregnant women aren't fat; they have a special glow about them."

Tune in to that glow. Regard your pregnancy as a time for showering your beloved with affection under exquisitely primordial circumstances. Barring medical complications, there is no reason to stop expressing your love abundantly. Making love is good for you *and* your unborn baby!

Suzanne Arms

Your relationship is the garden in which your child grows.

—Gayle Peterson

CHAPTER 7

DOWN THE HOMESTRETCH

The first couple of months, I hardly wanted to be home. It felt strange. Now, at seven months, I'm much more adjusted to the situation. We both just want to be together. We've got something that we both can concentrate on now. There's more of the idea of family, something to join us tightly together. I already feel it in our interactions with each other—a closer, more relaxed attitude.

BEGINNING AROUND THE SEVENTH MONTH OF PREGNANCY, partners begin returning home to each other with renewed enthusiasm and focus. A pregnant father now identifies more strongly with his new role. Relieved of the adjustment turmoil he has been grappling with for months, he senses a "freeing up," a "new flow of energy" directed toward his partner. The pregnant mother, too, feels increasingly more relaxed. More self-assured, she may sense an almost sublime at-oneness with her partner. Moving at last in much the same direction, the pregnant couple can together open their arms to the future: their child.

Togetherness

During the final three months of pregnancy, nearly all thoughts turn to the coming birth. Contemplating the event together, you can lay basic groundwork for a new alliance. Discussing your wishes, fears, and goals will promote a sense of security and comfort with each other and will solidify your determination to keep future events on track.

Tony, after six months of feeling distant from his wife and burdened by the stresses of becoming a father, remarks: "It's kind of an 'us' instead of an 'I'm here and you're there being pregnant' kind of thing. More of a partnership. There's been a turning in to each other in a more positive way almost all the time now." Visibly relieved to be feeling close again, he adds: "Walking around displaying the fact that you're going to have a child leaves you both open to anything—any kind of criticism or advice people feel like putting on you. At this time, it's easier to go to *each other*. The baby's brought us here together."

Feeling important and needed again is restorative. A man's hurts and resentments soon recede, whereupon appreciation and empathy surface with new intensity. In Juan's words: "It's hard for other people to 'get into' my partner's pregnancy. I see her in a real good light now, and I don't know that a lot of other people do. She's really vulnerable, and she needs me to turn to. I believe I'm the one person who she knows really understands her situation."

Drawing closer is a perfect balm for the anticipatory anxiety of the last trimester. Beginning around the seventh month of pregnancy, hundreds of urgent questions spring to mind and must await the

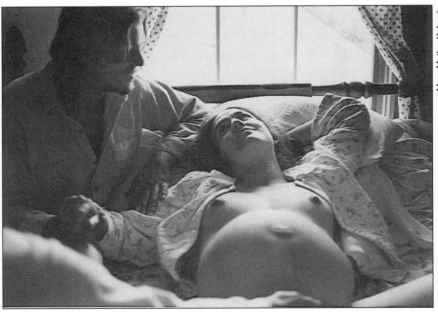

Mary Motley Kalergis

future for answers. Excitement mounts as thoughts and fantasies center on the birth. Time itself seems suspended. "Everything is unknown," says Jeff, eight and a half months pregnant. "You don't know when, how, or what it's going to be. So much of our time has been spent thinking, planning, imagining, waiting for the baby to be here. It's a great expectation, you could say. It's so close now, but I wish I could speed it up and make it come quicker!"

An expectant father can grow more nervous with each passing day, worrying about his ability to support his laboring partner and the possibility of labor complications, birth defects, or health problems. If feelings of alienation dominated his experience of early pregnancy, he may fear a "return to exile" after his baby is born. If he already has a child, he may wonder about his ability to support and care for another child.

A productive way to cope with anxieties about the unknown is to tackle the *known,* to begin tilling the soil for the coming birth. This, too, is best approached in partnership.

Preparing for Birth

As a father of the nineties, you can prepare for childbirth right along with your partner. Spurred on by the quickening and vitality of the third trimester, you can attend childbirth classes and discussion groups, build a support system of your own, help investigate a variety of birthing options, formulate a birthing philosophy, and define your parenting goals.

Childbirth Classes. Consider enrolling in childbirth classes, most of which are offered for four to eight consecutive weeks in early pregnancy and again in the seventh month. These classes can provide you with valuable information on fetal development, nutrition, maternal health, and the birthing process itself. Better yet, they can provide you with a forum for meeting other parents-in-waiting, sharing experiences, and gathering strategies and helpful suggestions.

Most couples find their childbirth classes beneficial. Women who attend with their partners, compared with those who do not, report reduced feelings of anxiety, fear, pain, and loneliness during labor, as well as more positive attitudes toward birthing. Men who attend classes, compared with those who do not, are more apt to feel helpful and needed during labor and more likely to see themselves as cocreators of life. Men who attend classes and participate in the birth do so with enhanced self-confidence and attunement; they also express heightened interest and satisfaction in contributing to family care during the months following childbirth.

Typically, today's childbirth educators are trained to disseminate information about birthing and to prepare the woman (and her partner if he is present) for labor and birth, *not* necessarily to attend to the psychological or interpersonal aspects of pregnancy and birth. Moreover, many well-trained educators recognize the need to encourage partner communication and the sharing of personal concerns, but are either reluctant to introduce these subjects without further training in counseling skills or unable to do so within the allotted time frame. Be sure to keep these points in mind when selecting a class to enroll in.

Childbirth Education Association (CEA), Lamaze (ASPO), and Bradley classes are offered in most major cities. To locate a childbirth educator experienced in these or other methods, look in the yellow pages, call local midwives or physicians, or check the bulletin boards at your natural food store (see appendix B). Before making a decision, interview each teacher. Ask about philosophy and goals, topics to be covered, class size, and whether or not you can meet with the teacher before or after scheduled sessions if you have important concerns that are not addressed in class.

One exciting option might be to arrange for individual classes tailored to your particular needs. If you and your partner, perhaps together with a small group of friends, would like to meet in the peace and quiet of your home, search for a childbirth educator who is willing to hold private classes and whose approach corresponds to your own.

Support Systems. Begin creating a support system for yourself so that you will not have to rely solely on your partner. Even one friend will do, provided that he or she is nurturing and nonjudgmental and will encourage you to talk about difficult feelings without trying to "fix" them. Look to friends (old and new) as well as members of your childbirth class or any group you belong to, or see about recruiting your childbirth teacher or perhaps one of your partner's friends. Together with your partner, make a list of your support crew, and keep it by the phone.

Birthing Options. If you and your partner have not yet decided on a place to birth, now is the time to give it thought. With family-centered births on the rise, a number of options are available. You may be attracted to the safety and intimacy of a midwife-assisted homebirth unimpeded by technology or drugs. Or you may prefer the homelike setting of a freestanding birth center staffed by midwives. Both choices lend themselves to sibling attendance as well as hospital transport and backup physician care should a complication arise.

Hospitals are beginning to offer variations on the high-tech, low-contact theme of former decades. Some allow for the presence of midwives; others provide a birthing room or an alternative birth center (ABC) room; a few are experimenting with doula care (round-the-clock woman-to-woman support from a trained labor coach). A growing number of hospitals allow fathers to assist in the birth of their children and permit father participation in cesareans. Rooming-in—an arrangement once reserved for mothers and babies—now accommodates fathers as well as siblings.

Take time to visit a few facilities. Even if you are planning to birth at home or at a birth center, you will want to select a hospital to use in the event of an emergency. Consider each visit an "interview." Check out the labor and delivery floor, the neonatal unit, the maternity ward. Acquaint yourself with the lay of the land, the policies, the protocols. In each setting, spend long, quiet moments determining whether or not this environment feels right for you.

If you and your partner have not yet decided on a birth practitioner—or if you have but are unhappy with the care you're receiving—think about the approach most likely to ease you through the concluding months of pregnancy and childbirth. Midwives, family practitioners, general practitioners, obstetricians, and obstetrician-gynecologists are all equipped to do the job well.

A *midwife* (defined as "with woman") will screen and assess your partner's health from pregnancy through the postpartum period, with a keen eye to nutrients, lifestyle, family dynamics, and extended support services. Midwives who receive their training through a hospital or university degree program are known as certi-fied nurse-midwives (CNMs); those who receive their training through private apprenticeship are known as direct-entry midwives. Midwives spend a great deal of time with clients and their families—far more than the obstetric standard—and in the event of high blood pressure, positive urinalysis results, or irregular uterine growth, will refer their clients to an obstetrician.

A *family practitioner* or *general practitioner* will also provide an obstetric referral should complications arise. A provider of this type may be able to offer a sense of familiarity and consistency of care, especially if this is someone you or your partner have been seeing for years. An *obstetrician*—highly specialized in problematic preg-nancies and routinized care—may be the practitioner of choice in the presence of, or fear of, complications.

A Birth Plan of Your Own. Before deciding on the person who will usher you across the threshold of birth, take some time to set out your *own* birthing philosophy. What factors are most important to you? What role do you want to play? Once you have a clear idea of your desires, exchange philosophies with your partner. Then together, draw up a birth plan.

The plan that you and your partner arrive at will help you determine which practitioner is best for you. Be sure to interview several candidates. Get a feel for the receptivity, availability, and responsiveness of each one. (Are you encouraged to ask questions? Are your questions answered clearly?) Bring to each interview a list of your concerns, and address them all. Do not be intimidated; as a consumer, you are entitled to query every aspect of the care you and your newborn will receive. Realize that some health profes-sionals will be more than willing to arrange for hands-on father participation in birth if you state your request directly.

Leave each interview with a list of families the practitioner has cared for in recent months. Consider contacting each family to get a sense of client satisfaction. The doctor or midwife you ultimately engage should be someone with a good reputation and the ability to support you *as a couple.*

YOUR PHILOSOPHY OF CHILDBIRTH

To formulate a birthing philosophy, reflect on the following questions:

- Do you want the services of a midwife, a family practitioner, a general practitioner, or an obstetrician?
- Do you want to be included in office visits?
- What type of birth do you want—a homebirth, a birth center birth, or a hospital birth?
- Which hospital would most suit your needs?
- If you have a practitioner already in mind, with which hospital is he or she affiliated? Will this person provide you with information about local childbirth classes and parenting classes? Will he or she recommend a pediatrician or pediatric nurse practitioner with whom you can meet before or immediately after the birth? What contingency plans will be in place if your practitioner cannot attend the birth?
- How do you envision your ideal birth environment?
- What are your thoughts about pain and pain control? Who do you think should decide on the need for anesthesia in labor and birth—you, your partner, the practitioner?
- What do you think about electronic fetal monitoring, restricted movement, and food and drink limitations during labor?
- Do you feel strongly about the use of anesthesia, forceps, gentle birth techniques, induced labor, routine episiotomies, father participation in birth, sibling attendance at birth, or rooming-in?
- How soon after birth do you want to hold your infant? For how long? What if a cesarean is needed?
- Do you want your newborn to breastfeed before being whisked off to the newborn nursery? Do you want to take your child to the nursery yourself?
- Do you want to be informed in advance of any procedures that will be performed on your child (shots, vaccines, genetic tests) and to retain your right to informed consent or refusal?

The Other Side of Involvement

The trend in perinatal care is to encourage—and sometimes push—fathers into more active involvement. For some men, this is a welcomed push. For others, it is not. More than a few men enter childbirth classes, practitioners' offices, and birthing rooms reluctantly, if not resentfully.

These men are not quite sure that childbirth is for them. And with good reason. Despite our culture's recent acceptance of fathers at birth, childbirth is still regarded as a ceremony between the child-bearing woman and her care provider. The prevailing medical model has prohibited family involvement for so long that a man may unwittingly "relinquish" his partner to the physician or midwife rather than insist on taking part in the birth of his child. Intimidation is at work as well. The exclusionary obstetric practices enforced for decades give the impression that men other than trained medical

---

PARTICIPATION QUESTIONS FOR PREGNANT FATHERS

Before taking part in any aspect of the coming birth, be clear about your intentions:

- Are you going to classes, prenatal visits, or the birth itself against your will? If so, why?

- Are you going just to please your partner? If so, why?

- Are you going in an effort to patch up relationship troubles?

- Are you going because you think you should? If so, why?

- Are you stubbornly refusing to take part? Are you giving your partner a hard time? If so, why?

- Are you being honest and direct with your partner? If not, why? What are you afraid of?

personnel overreact to, interfere with, or mishandle the events of labor and birth—that fathers, in other words, are superfluous. Too often, such presumptions seep into the minds of childbearing couples.

If you are participating reluctantly in childbirth preparations, be sure to discuss the situation with your partner. If you do not want to attend the birth, try to explain the real reasons for your objection. Neither your silence nor your unwilling attendance can be helpful to her. In fact, if you are not open and honest about your sentiments, your presence will most likely *increase* the tension and pressure she is already feeling.

If, on the other hand, you sense that your partner does not want you at the birth, check out your intuition with her. *You could be correct.* She may be embarrassed about birthing in your presence, about being naked, exposed, and in pain. She may be frightened or insecure, afraid of revealing her feelings or worried about

---

PARTICIPATION QUESTIONS FOR PREGNANT MOTHERS

Before encouraging or discouraging your partner's participation in any aspect of the coming birth, clarify your attitudes and feelings:

- How do you really feel about having him participate in classes, prenatal visits, labor, birth? Are you comfortable or uncomfortable when you think of him being there?

- Are you harboring resentment and hostility toward your partner? If so, why? How are you expressing it?

- Are you pushing him away? Are you trying to spite him? If so, why? Is this behavior satisfying? Does it get you what you want?

- Have you told your partner honestly and directly how you are feeling about him? If not, why? What are you afraid of?

letting you down in some way. Or—and here's the clincher—she may not want you there because she is *angry* and *distrustful of you*. Perhaps she has come to see you as uninvolved, or unavailable and not really wanting the baby.

If you and your partner are in serious conflict, now is certainly the time to clear the air. Seek out trusted friends to help you uncover the problems and talk about them. If tension and misunderstanding persist, obtain advice from your care provider or a professional therapist. This is a *crucial stage* in your relationship. The time you take to clarify confusion now will pay off later, in years of joyful involvement with your family.

Miguel Pisarro

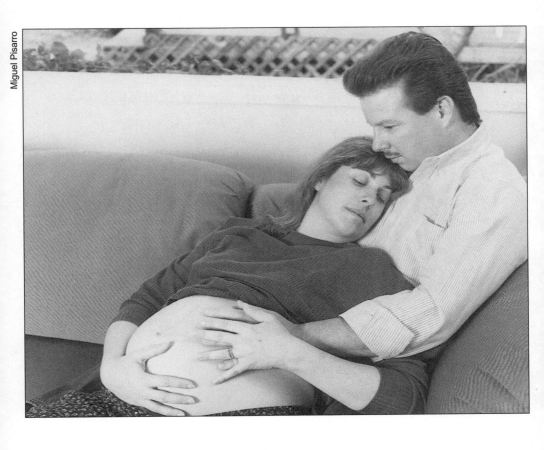

Once you tell somebody the way that you feel, you can feel it begin to ease. . . . Shower the people you love with love. Show them the way that you feel. Things are going to be much better if you only will.

—James Taylor
"Shower the People"

CHAPTER 8

PARTNER-TO-PARTNER COMMUNICATION

She keeps thinking that I'm attacking her when I'm not. I'm just trying to let her know how I feel. But she insists that I'm angry and critical of her. What can I say? I'm so frustrated. I can't get through to her. I don't know if it's me or her. . . . We need some new way of talking or something, 'cause I'm doing everything I know how to and it's not working.

THERE ARE NO "POSITIVE" OR "NEGATIVE" EMOTIONS, no right or wrong ways to feel. There are, however, effective ways of addressing our feelings and communicating our needs to the people we love.

The transition to parenthood is a deeply personal psychological process that demands our unflagging attention. We can ignore our experiences and become swept up in the changes around us, or we can be mindful of events taking place within and around us. Choosing to remain self-aware, we awaken to our inner world and become more sensitive and receptive to others, more expressive, and better able to strengthen our partner bond.

New communication tools are needed. Old standbys must be honed. Properly equipped, we can become consummate communicators capable of shaping and smoothing a truly happy union. Practice is essential. Skillfulness will follow. Improvement is guaranteed.

Toward Self-Knowing

To communicate effectively, we must enter the inner world of feelings and needs. Stepping through the portal of awareness into the realm of emotions, we stumble upon pieces of ourselves that have been laying dormant since early childhood. In taking up and waking up these remnants of psyche, we begin feeling more "in touch," more complete. Slices of life we never before noticed capture our interest and imagination. We feel fuller and more alive. Increasingly cognizant of our own inner sensations, we experience *other* people with greater clarity, certainty, and enjoyment. From this vantage point, we begin expanding and enlivening our relationships.

Entering the world of emotions takes a willingness to venture into the unfamiliar—a hero's journey. If you have already stepped through the gateway by listening to your unique responses to pregnancy, I congratulate you and encourage you to add the following itinerary to your journey.

Awareness Exercise 1: Meditation

This exercise lends itself to taping for repeated listening. Also try reading it to your partner, perhaps taking turns as reader and listener—it's good medicine for both of you, for it facilitates heightened relaxation, clarity, and a new appreciation of feelings and needs.

- Sit alone quietly and comfortably, in a peaceful setting. Close your eyes, and take a few deep, cleansing breaths. Focus on your body sensations—your breathing, your heartbeat.

- Notice the thoughts and images that come to your attention. (For a time, nothing may announce itself. That, too, is fine. Don't force yourself to experience anything in particular; simply be aware of *what is.*) Allow whatever awareness is present to come in, move through you, then out. Stay with the flow, avoiding the temptation to interrupt or modify the thoughts that come. Just relax, breathing slowly, deeply, comfortably.

- Notice how easily one awareness moves into the next, how calming this natural rhythm is. Take all the time you need to relax into your rhythm.

- When you feel rested and satisfied, slowly open your eyes. Spend a few minutes reorienting yourself to the light and other external stimuli before continuing your day.

You may want to discuss your meditation experience with your partner. You may instead prefer to track it in the privacy of a journal, put a new awareness into action, or alter an old, unfulfilling habit or routine. Or you may simply wish to savor the delectable sense of restfulness and centeredness, reserving implementation for another day.

Awareness Exercise 2: Scanning Your Interests and Preferences

Having worked with couples over the past twenty-five years, I have heard a multitude of men and women remark: "I don't know who I am anymore. I've given all of me to him (her)." The best antidote I have found for this relationship dilemma is to tune in to personal likes (and dislikes), interests (and indifferences), and preferences (and aversions). We all have likes and dislikes, things we would rather do or not do. So often, however, we sublimate these desires in the quest for harmony and confluence in our close relationships.

This exercise will ease you back to yourself. Try it wherever you happen to be, whether at home, in a park, or on the job.

- Position yourself comfortably, and attend to your breath. Breathe gently and deeply. Relax. Look around slowly, and stop when something catches your attention. What is it about this object that attracts you—its color, shape, scent, pitch, texture? Take note of this quality.

- Scan your surroundings once again until something else draws your interest. Do you like what you see (hear, smell) or not? Determine exactly how this object affects you—whether you like it or not, and why ("I like this painting because it's vibrant," or "It's too bright," or "It's too sloppy"). Don't be wishy-washy. Let yourself have an opinion.

- Repeat the exercise until you have identified your responses to at least five objects in your environment.

Awareness Exercise 3: Reviewing the Day's Events

- Reflect on the events of your day. Recall at least one experience that you enjoyed (showering, eating, a task, an interaction). Recall at least one experience that you did not enjoy.

- What bored you today? What stimulated you? What pleased you? What annoyed or frustrated you?

- Which interactions were important and meaningful to you? Which were not? What accounts for these differences?

- Who are you eager to see again? Who would you rather avoid? Why?

- Are you left with any lingering thoughts or feelings from your day—things you wish you had said or done, but didn't? If so, what are these echoes telling you?

Based on insights you have gleaned from the previous three exercises, state your preferences, likes, and dislikes in your present life situation. Do not analyze or judge your statements—they are your truths at this time. It is your right to like or dislike circumstances as well as people's behavior and attitudes. You are entitled to your feelings, interests, and preferences.

Awareness Exercise 4: Taking Stock of Your Partnership

- Think about your relationship with your partner. What do you especially appreciate about your partner? What do you enjoy doing together? What don't you enjoy doing? What bothers you about your partner? How do you feel leaving, greeting, conversing with, being near, and being alone with your partner?

- Think about specific times you spent together over the past week. Did you feel understood, appreciated, attended to, or overlooked? Did you feel loved, discounted, or rejected? In response, were you calm, tense, secure, insecure, angry, annoyed, happy, resentful, or hurt? The following format may help you clarify your feelings:

  When my partner said (did) _____, I felt _____.
  What I did (said) in response was _____.
  What I wanted to do (say) was _____.

- If you did not say what you wanted to at the time or soon thereafter, try this exercise: *Imagine your partner sitting nearby and listening attentively to you. Imagine yourself speaking comfortably about whatever is on your mind, then about whatever you most want your partner to hear about your feelings. Now think about what you most want to ask of your partner; imagine yourself asking for it and enjoying a satisfying outcome.* These imaginative forays will give you a chance to air your feelings while anticipating a positive response. It may be just the boost you need to be more assertive with your partner the next time something significant comes up.

Awareness Exercise 5: Turning Off Your Self-Censor

- Think about the opinions, sentiments, or concerns you ordinarily censor while speaking with your partner, including the "little things" you keep inside for one reason or another. What are you most reluctant to talk about? What do you suppose might happen if you brought it up? What has happened in the past when you shared serious concerns with your partner, your parents, your friends? If you were not well received, ask yourself: Is this the same type of situation as before? If it isn't, are the chances of getting a more positive response better *this* time?

- When you express yourself freely and spontaneously, do you feel heard, understood, responded to?

- When you censor yourself, what is your attitude toward your partner—tentative, distant, resentful? Do you express these feelings directly or indirectly?

Censored material may seem inconsequential in the moment. When suppressed for too long, however, it converts to unfinished business and leads to large-scale difficulties. To avoid major relationships problems, strive to bring your feelings out.

Awareness Exercise 6: Tapping in to Mumblings, Grumblings, and Body Language

- Listen to the monologue that runs through your mind during the day when you're not concentrating on a task, and at night before you doze off to sleep.

- Pay attention to the pictures you show yourself—the fleeting images that pass through your mind.

- Notice when your body tenses up; when you are bored, tired, anxious, or achy. Observe what you are thinking and doing at these times. If you are with someone or have recently left an encounter, take note of your body sensations. Is your neck saying, "This is a pain in the neck," or your stomach saying, "I can't stomach any more of this," or your tapping foot saying, "Let's get out of here"? Or is your renewed energy or lightness saying, "This feels good"?

The above exercise will provide you with cues for listening to your body. Use them to get a firm handle on your inner promptings.

Awareness Exercise 7: Recording Your Wants

- Make a list of the things you want. Begin with those you are certain of (a nice home, a vacation, a dinner out) and move on to those that pertain to your relationship. Be concrete: write "I want you to listen to me" rather than "I want you to care," or "I want a hug" rather than "I want some attention."

- Share your list with your partner. A direct statement such as "I want to go out with you tonight" or "I really want to talk with you" can open the door to enhanced communication.

Effective Listening

We all want to be understood by and to better understand the people we care about; yet few of us have been taught how to receive or send clear messages. What do you do, for example, when you sense that your partner is upset? Unsure of what the problem is, do you probe, guess, or ignore the situation? If your goal is to make contact, your best course of action is to listen and respond in ways that will *encourage her to reveal her underlying feelings and needs.*

Effective listening is a rare and beautiful commodity in today's busy world. The path of good intentions, however, is teeming with pitfalls.

The Eager Beaver Pitfall (Halfheartedness). Trying to be attentive when you are not genuinely available to listen spells trouble. If your heart is not open, your ears won't be either. So if you are preoccupied, frustrated, or too tired to really listen, wait. Request a rain check. Tell your partner that you *do* want to be attentive to her but now is just not a good time. Let her know when a better time would be. Then slow down, make that important phone call, blow off some steam, or do whatever you need to so that you can be receptive.

The White Knight Pitfall (Advising, Giving Solutions). Your job is *not* to solve your partner's problems, rescue her from uncomfortable situations, or "make" her feel better. Rescuing and advising at best offer only temporary distractions. The White Knight, well-intentioned as he may be, diverts his partner from attending to her underlying feelings and mastering situations on her own. The more he atttempts to solve her problems or salve her feelings, the more resistance he will encounter. Resentful of the intrusion, she may protest, "Please, I'd rather do it myself!" or "You wouldn't suggest that if you understood how *I* feel." In effect, the White Knight needs to realize that his true mission is to create a safe setting so that his partner will feel comfortable expressing herself. This is best accomplished by conveying *trust* in her ability to take care of herself and *respect* for her individual pace and style.

The Moralist Pitfall (Dispensing Shoulds, Musts, Warnings). Preaching will surely cause your partner to cringe, emotionally if not physically. Her unuttered response is apt to be something like: "Don't tell me what I should or shouldn't do. You're not my parent. I'm not a child. I have my own conscience, thank you. Get away— I don't need this." Having had our fill of mandates and dire predictions from parents, teachers, relatives, and society, we do not take kindly to hearing more stultifying directives as adults.

The Shrink Pitfall (Explaining, Interrogating, Interpreting, Asking Why). Your partner may abhor being told what she feels or why she does what she does. When you attempt to explain her motives according to your assumptions, she is apt to feel misunderstood ("Don't lay that on me"), pathologized, or uncertain of herself. If you approach her with "Why don't you ever_____?" or "Why do you always _____?" she may shut down altogether. "Why" questions often feel like interrogations and put the listener immediately on the defensive. If nothing else, try replacing each "why" with a "what."

The Critical Parent Pitfall (Judging, Blaming, Lecturing, Name-Calling). Beware of accusations and injunctions such as "How could you feel (do) that?" "You always (never) _____," "That's bad (good, right, wrong)," and "You're lazy (selfish, a nag, immature)." These landmines can only damage your communication efforts, for their underlying message is, "You're not OK. I know better." Comments of this sort may flash your partner back to childhood when her behavior, if not her identity, may have been judged, criticized, or punished.

The Pollyanna Pitfall (Discounting, Denying, Belittling). Steer clear of invalidating pronouncements such as "You don't really mean (feel, think) that, do you?" "You'll feel better tomorrow. Forget about it," "It's not really that bad," and "You're just upset (tired, having a bad day)." "You" questions and statements point the finger and may push your partner either away from her experience or away from you.

Effective Responses. Constructive replies will emerge when you convey interest in listening to a problem and understanding it. Any verbal or nonverbal response that relays this message will promote better contact.

Effective responses often come in the form of *facilitators,* such as "What's happening, hon? You look beat. Do you want to talk?" "Uh-huh, I see. I'm with you," "Really? Tell me more about it," "How was that for you?" "When was that?" "Hmmm . . . interesting," and "I'm sorry you're hurting." Facilitators, unlike the snares noted above, do not interfere with the expression of feelings. On the contrary, they encourage conversation by inviting the speaker to disclose the difficulty.

Effective listening also hinges on *reflecting feelings*—listening "between the words" to hear what the speaker is experiencing. Foraging for the essential feeling-message your partner is trying to convey can be like plunging the subterranean depths to capture a pearl. Her surface message may be: "Gosh, I've gained only ten pounds. And I haven't felt the baby move. Jane's gained at least fifteen pounds already, and her baby's kicking all the time." The deeper message could be "I'm worried (concerned, feeling insecure)" *or* "I'm feeling alone and different" *or* "I really need some reassurance from you."

Or her surface message may be: "It seems our two year old is always crying. I just don't know what to do about it." The deeper message in this instance could be "I'm really frustrated (irritated)" *or* "I'm afraid I'm not an effective parent" *or* "I'm feeling upset, scared, and unsure of myself" *or* "I'd really like your help with this."

To reflect feelings, you must *suspend all personal associations with the statement you hear.* Cleared of your assumptions, listen closely to what the speaker is saying, then attempt to send back the underlying message as accurately as possible: "Are you saying that _____?" or "It sounds like you feel _____ about _____."

If your feedback rings true, your partner will feel heard—a sure incentive to continue talking. If your feedback misses the mark, no harm has been done; she can set you straight ("No, that's not it. It's more like _____"), rephrasing her statement until she does feel

---

FACILITATING WITH YOUR PARTNER

- You assume the role of sender. Your partner assumes the role of listener. As sender, choose an issue or problem you wish to talk about. Take five minutes or so to share your thoughts and feelings on the matter. All the while, your partner, as listener, responds *only with facilitators* in a variety of innovative ways.

- Switch roles, and repeat the exercise.

- Tell your partner one thing she as a listener did that you appreciated, and have her do the same for you.

REFLECTING FEELINGS WITH YOUR PARTNER

To practice reflecting back your partner's feelings, try this exercise, taking turns as sender and listener:

The sender issues a surface message without revealing the deeper feeling content until the listener indicates some level of understanding. The listener, meanwhile, tries a variety of approaches to capture the sender's feeling. As the challenge mounts, the listener uses facilitators or restates the message, whatever it takes to sustain the dialogue until the deeper message is revealed.

Here is one couple's experience with this exercise.

> SENDER: I spoke to my mother again, and she just went on and on about her gardening and about Dad's heart condition.
>
> LISTENER *[trying a facilitator]:* It sounds like she's concerned about your father's health. Are *you?*
>
> SENDER: That's not it. It's that my mother and I were talking, and she just went on and on about her gardening and about Dad's health.
>
> LISTENER *[trying another facilitator]:* Is it that your mother is irritating you?
>
> SENDER: Not exactly. I called her up and she just went on and on about their stuff.
>
> LISTENER *[restating the message in his own words]:* She just went on and on when you called her?
>
> SENDER: Yes, she's so wrapped up in herself and him. She hasn't visited me or even asked about the pregnancy.
>
> *[Deeper message revealed]*

understood. Combing through the richly diversified world of feelings is a labor of love. Let patience and perseverance be your allies.

Many couples report that the more proficient they become at reflecting feelings, the more dissatisfied they are making assumptions, jumping to conclusions, and offering unsolicited advice. And the better understood they feel in their day-to-day conversations.

Clear and Honest Self-Expression

How do couples express important emotions effectively? First, by being aware of their feelings. Second, by identifying them. Third, by establishing a climate safe for sharing. And finally, by coming forth honestly and frequently, straight from the heart.

Speaking the truth. Blurred messages produce static and confusion. They come in the shape of *disguised wishes* (asking "What do you want to do?" in lieu of asserting "I want to _____") and *denied desires* (saying "It doesn't matter to me" when it really does). These common forms of exchange obscure the real message, which is: "My desire (opinion, feeling) is _____."

To avoid sending blurred messages, check to see if there are statements hiding beneath the questions you ask. There may very well be. If so, try changing "why" questions into "I" statements. Also replace "I have to" when you mean "I *choose* to" or "I *want* to," "I can't" when you mean "I *won't*" or "I *don't want* to." In addition, convert "you" statements into "I" statements. These alterations are not mere syntactic maneuvers; they indicate that you are accepting responsibility for how you feel, what you do, and how you are affected by others.

Being honest means revealing the truth about everything— which may very well include the desire to be alone. Do not refrain from expressing this wish for fear of hurting your partner's feelings. She, too, may want some time alone. And avoid subscribing to the notion that the happy couple wants to do everything together. This dangerous misconception can squeeze the individuality out of *any* partnership. Free to choose your times of separateness and togetherness, you will strengthen your relationship, deepen your appreciation for each other, and indeed be a happier couple.

Spending Time Together. If you are not coming together spontaneously and joyfully on a regular basis, schedule a block of hours each week for "dating" or for time together at home. Planning, as unromantic as it sounds, can preserve the closeness you will both want and need in the challenging months ahead.

During your "together time," share confidences. When was the last time you let your partner in on a deep, dark secret, or revealed a hidden aspect of your life? Whispered secrets are magical, as are never-before-uttered stories of childhood adventure, mischief, accomplishment, and rebellion.

To reminisce is to relive the past in preparation for the future. So dig out the dusty legends. Tell your partner what you were like as a child, what your mom and dad were like, how they got along,

---

FIRST ME, THEN YOU (AND VICE VERSA)

- Spend five minutes saying everything you want to say, *uninterrupted* by your partner. (If it's hard getting started, let yourself fumble around until things come into focus. Don't rush. This is time very well spent.) Nothing is off-limits, so complain, whine, vent, and free-associate to your heart's content.

- For the next five minutes, let your partner say everything she wants to say. Remember, no interrupting. Just listen and take it all in.

This simple exercise provides a safe context in which to "clear out" your disturbances and be heard. One expectant father, after trying this exercise for the first time, exclaimed: "I didn't realize so much was on my mind." His partner commented, "I had no idea *you* were feeling and dealing with so much." Light is shed, plus the rare opportunity for expressing yourself without interruption or reaction is therapeutic and capable of generating surprising solutions.

how they treated you and your siblings, who your heroes and heroines were, and what your important relationships were like. Add drama, or simply weave your tales.

In the process, you might uncover a few tales to tell your child some day. You might even decide to establish "personal storytime" as a family ritual. Beyond stories, share dreams, ideal and catastrophic fantasies, hopes, and fears—the stuff close families are made of.

"Coming Out" with Desires and Expectations. The entry into parenthood awakens hopes we hold for ourselves, our partners, and our children. If you learned as a child to keep your desires and expectations to yourself, you may be inclined to keep your current ones hidden as well. Closeted, however, they can take a heavy toll on your relationship, sparking bitterness and resentment when they suddenly do pour forth, or loneliness and depression while sequestered within.

Desires and expectations need a regular "airing out." To gear up for good aeration, ask yourself two questions: "What do I want from my partner now?" and "What am I willing (not willing) to give right now?" Then share what you have found hiding in your closet, and clean house together.

Start articulating important expectations before your baby arrives by asking directly for what you want. If you feel reluctant or particularly uncomfortable expecting your partner to do something for you, much less *asking* her to, think back on the patterning you received in early childhood. How did your siblings and parents respond when you asked for attention or anything else you very much wanted? Were you ignored, put down, diverted from your goal, told to stop being greedy, sent to your room, hit? Realize that the punitive treatment you were subjected to then has shaped your present uneasiness about asking and receiving, but has little to do with your present life situation: *your partner is likely to respond to your requests very differently than your parents did.*

Parenting will be a full-time job replete with responsibilities. Old, established give-and-take routines will change substantially. In preparation for the time ahead, imagine what it will be like to have an infant in your home. What new demands will be placed on you and your partner? Who will feed, bathe, and dress the baby? Who will put the baby to bed and get up in the middle of the night with baby? Who will change and wash the diapers? Who will cook, clean, shop, run errands? Who will be in charge of greeting visitors and fielding calls from relatives and friends? How much time off from work will you each be requesting? Whose needs will take priority— yours, your partner's, your child's? When and how will you find time for yourself and each other?

List the tasks that might arise, then sit down with your partner and divide them equitably. Formulate a preliminary agreement; you can always revise it as unforeseen responsibilities emerge, or decide to swap jobs as time goes on. The point is that arrangements made collaboratively before baby's arrival form a foundation for a stronger partnership alliance and serve as a prototype for future *family* decision making.

Agreeing to Disagree. Another popular misconception is that happy couples don't fight. Let's debunk this one once and for all. Not only is it unrealistic to expect agreement on all fronts, but too much agreement can lead to stagnation and codependence. A relationship without conflict is a relationship devoid of passion as well. So agree to disagree, and let your rapture flow.

Consenting to Time Out. Conflict can get out of hand, especially when hurts and resentments have been brewing and communication has reached a standstill. If and when disagreeing turns toxic and hurtful, call a time-out. The rules are simple: only one person need request the break, after which the conflicting parties agree to separate and meet at a prearranged time to try again.

Communing without Words. Words often fail to convey the heart's message. At times, nothing is more revealing than a warm smile, a loving touch, an understanding glance, an embrace, a lap to be playful in, or a shoulder to cry on. The currents of love speak powerfully in silence.

Occasions will arise when you and your partner will want to remember that nonverbal communication is a powerful medium. When, where, and how do you feel best being together without talking—watching videos, listening to music, dancing, cuddling, working on different projects in separate rooms, working side by side? Relishing in more of these good times now may convince you never to forfeit them.

Remember, too, that the language of touch can transcend all words. How, when, and where do you enjoy touching (being touched) and caressing (being caressed)? Indulge in a full-body massage to soothe away tension. Take turns massaging each other. Let your fingers speak of love; let your skin—the external nervous system—answer to the strokes of your loved one, transforming feelings of separateness into an experience of union. As renowned anthropologist Ashley Montagu writes, in his classic work *Touch,* "The healing power of touch is beyond our wildest dreams."[23]

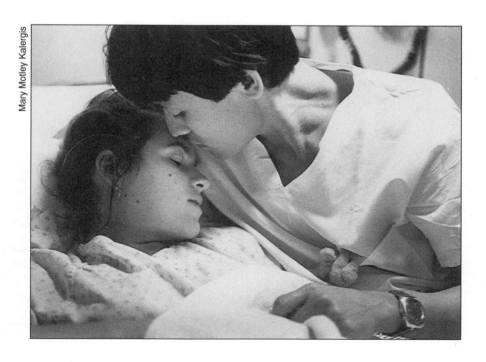

Mary Motley Kalergis

Birth is love made visible.

—Paul Brenner

CHAPTER 9

LABORING AND BIRTHING TOGETHER

I'll never forget those first moments. The best word for what I felt as she birthed him was reverence. *I instinctively removed my shirt and slowly, carefully drew him to my body. I touched and counted each finger and toe, then closed my eyes, swayed, and rocked him into my life. Never have I felt so quiet and at peace, so humbled yet powerful and full . . . thanking God.*

LABOR AND BIRTH CARRY A FATHER-IN-WAITING through a crescendo of emotions. After the initial excitement of checking in to the hospital, or contacting the midwife and arranging the birth setting, things can get mysteriously quiet. Time moves slowly. Questions flood the mind: Am I prepared for this? Will I be helpful? Will my partner get through everything all right? Will there be complications? Will our baby be healthy and intact? Will we have a boy or a girl? Twins?

The expectant father's attention shifts back and forth between concern for his laboring partner's well-being and anxiety about his capability as a birth partner and a new father. Tense with apprehension and anticipation, and having run out of things to do, he may look for reassurance—a smile of recognition, a touch on the shoulder, a task to perform. His partner, however, is clearly engaged in a task of her own. And so the realization dawns that he must pretty much fend for himself, at least until the next wave of activity begins to crest.

The Call to Labor

The onset of regular contractions can propel a very expectant father into a state of agitation. External events and internal responses build to a new pitch and, orchestrated entirely by nature, appear to leave little room for human intercession.

The Outer Reality. For a man accustomed to *performing,* labor can be exasperating, because it is hard to know just what to *do.* Here are some ideas that, when implemented with your partner's consent and guidance, may prove helpful to everyone concerned. Replenish your partner's supply of food and drinks (keeping an eye on your blood sugar levels as well). Rub her back, pressing hard with your knuckles to knead away lower back pain. Offer her your chest, arms, or shoulder as a resting place. Rearrange the pillows comfortably and prepare soothing compresses. Offer nipple stimulation to accelerate labor. Between contractions, take walks together. During contractions, offer to support her in a standing-lean position; embrace her; if she wants to squat, hold her up under the arms. Also feel free to take well-deserved breaks when other care-

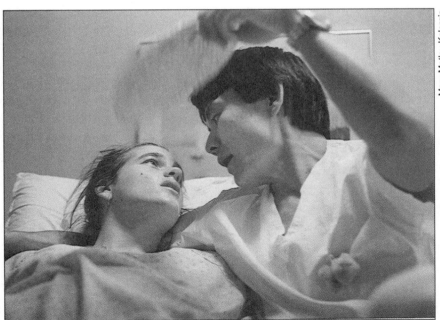

Mary Motley Kalergis

Teri Preston

givers are on the scene. Aside from these activities, the most helpful thing you can do at this point is wait—with focused attention.

Despite common parlance, you are not a labor coach; you are a
labor partner. As such, your primary task is not to *perform* or to
accomplish some result, but to *be*—to be alert to your partner's
needs, trusting in her process and her competence, willing to follow
her instructions, and prepared to help her attend fully to her body's
signals. *Her body knows exactly what to do.*

Your special importance lies in loving your partner, caring for
her, and helping her labor in peace by keeping the environment
clear of unnecessary intrusions. This means stepping in as her advocate whenever the need arises. *Vigilance is a must.* Negotiate any
disputes that may arise between your partner and the medical staff.
Take care of the paperwork. Redirect discouraging comments. Insist
that all procedures get your final OK. (Are they truly necessary? Are
they in keeping with your birth plan and your partner's wishes?
Although she may be in no position to think analytically at this
point, you can present her with the options and back her preferences.) Attending to your partner in the prebirth hours is a way of
nurturing her, your child, and yourself.

The Swell of Emotions. Male participants describe labor as encompassing the most wonderful and awesome moments in their lives. Anticipation, worry, and tension can build to overwhelming proportions, often eclipsing surges of excitement about meeting the long-awaited baby. As one father puts it: "I was very eager to just get that baby down there and out—to get it all over with, to see my child. All our fears and hopes were right on the surface. We were about to find out what kind of baby we were going to have!"

You, too, may experience your part in labor as a mixed blessing. Closer than ever to your partner, your child, and the moment of birth, you will also be very near the pain and turbulence of this extraordinary event. Anger or resentment may unexpectedly arise, particularly if you are in a hospital and the staff separates you from your partner upon admission, during examinations, or en route to the delivery room. Broken contact at any of these junctures can leave you feeling extraneous and quite miffed. You may encounter assorted red tape as well, or overworked, irritable nurses and seemingly needless procedures. In each case, tenacity and tact are of the essence. Express your displeasure, yet be careful to avoid alienating hospital personnel—not an easy feat at such a stressful time. Still, civility is essential, because the last thing you will want to do is generate tension and hostility around the birth.

As labor progresses, questions may loom large. Lou recalls: "I was concerned about how I would react to watching my wife give birth. Everything was on the line. It was important to do it right. It was my responsibility to guide her through this the way I hoped to and the way she needed me to—to help her relax and enjoy." You, like Lou, may be uneasy about your role in the advanced stages of labor. You may wonder: Will I be able to ease my partner's pain? Will I know how to help her? Can I bear to see her bleeding? Anytime you feel wracked with doubts, remember that labor participation does *not* test your ability to help. Nor does your performance as a labor partner in any way reflect your ability to love, either as a mate or as a father.

Another onerous question that may move front and center is: Will the baby be a boy or a girl? One new father explains: "In the beginning, I didn't really think about our baby's gender. When things got down to the wire there in the labor room, these thoughts

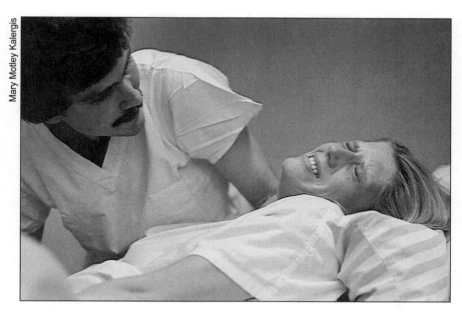

Mary Motley Kalergis

kept pouring in. . . . Both my partner and I had said that having a girl wouldn't make any difference to us. Afterward, though, we both realized it had made a great deal of difference. We were both disappointed she wasn't a boy."

Giving voice to gender preferences has been considered taboo. Nevertheless, as about-to-be parents, we often do harbor hopes for a boy or girl child. Our emotional investment in our child's gender may reveal itself in fantasies or dreams during pregnancy, or in disappointment after the birth. So try not to condemn yourself for stumbling upon a hidden gender preference while awaiting the birth of your baby, or for feeling disgruntled afterward if your gender dreams do not come true. Your wishes are perfectly natural, and your disappointment is bound to dissolve as you begin establishing a close, loving relationship with your child.

Steve, a new father, spent his pregnancy enthusiastically awaiting the birth of a son. He talked endlessly about playing basketball and football with his boy, being a "special buddy" to him, and doing things he missed out on with his own father. When Lyndie was born, Steve circumvented his disappointment and focused fully on his gratitude for having a healthy child. Only weeks later did he express his dismay—and his underlying concerns about fathering a little girl. "I definitely have a more conservative responsibility in bringing up a daughter," he said. "I can see myself being really worried when she goes out on her first date, for instance. Unless boys have changed a lot since I was a teenager, I'm not too thrilled about the whole dating prospect. All I know about is from the boy's point of view. What do I know about being a girl and about raising one? I think I'm going to be awfully protective of Lyndie."

Alongside the raw emotions and discomforting questions precipitated by labor are some compelling relationship needs. More than anything else, men need to feel important and effective, valued and wanted. Elliot describes his experience in these words: "Joyce was needing a lot of me—I could tell by the way she looked at me and squeezed my hand. I was so glad to be able to give myself to her. What mattered wasn't what I was doing physically or materially, but rather my love and caring. I felt that I needed nothing from her, that my good thoughts were being received and were helping her. There was some sort of extrasensory communication going on between us."

If your efforts to help are not validated by your partner or her other caregivers, you may feel alienated from the events of labor. As Bob says: "Even though I was there participating, I felt kind of helpless just watching her suffer through the pain and unable to physically do anything about it. I felt kind of useless much of the time— more like an observer than a participant."

Feelings of helplessness and isolation are sometimes *brought into* the labor room by men who see themselves as unimportant to the pregnancy or who feel insecure as partners or caregivers. These feelings are often rooted in irrational guilt ("I'm putting her through all this," "I did this to her") compounded by unrealistic expectations about pain in labor.

Guilt pangs need not accompany men to the labor room. Perinatal professionals can help keep expectations realistic by informing pregnant couples about the etiology, duration, intensity, and management of pain; showing films of true-to-life births; and inviting follow-up discussion. By the same token, knowing what labor pain *was* like and that his presence offered relief can help a new father ward off lingering pangs of self-reproach.

Feelings of culpability are least likely to arise when men participate fully in labor. John, a homebirther, recalls: "When I was with Ellen, I felt so close, so involved with her feelings. It was like I was experiencing with her—almost *in myself*—what she was going through. I couldn't actually feel the pain, but in my heart I was feeling for her. Sometimes I had to step away from the intensity to stay with *me*."

Labor engineers an ineluctable upsurge of emotions certain to rattle the most steadfast participants. As the accelerating waves of contractions peak and subside before your eyes—and ears— remember that there is no such thing as an "ideal labor partner." Be as present as you can be. Let your love shine through. Welcome the experience, savor it, and enjoy the crowning glory of your baby's birth.

Initiated by Childbirth

A man is initiated into fatherhood through his involvement in the birth process. While participating in birth, he begins forging lifelong fathering memories as well as a personal template for future bonding. His partnership, becoming more deeply cast, takes on inexplicable dimensions. Indeed, birthing together may be the most intimate act a man and woman can engage in. The event itself, however, provides no opportunity for such telescopic understandings.

The power of the emotions aroused by his baby's emergence can leave a man dazed. In Keith's words: "It was like being in suspension—a state of shock. Gosh, if I had had to be actually doing the birth, I would have been in trouble. It's like I was there watching it, but almost outside my body."

Beneath the daze is a wellspring of inspiration. Childbirth, according to one new father, is profoundly *spiritual:* "The fact is that in a matter of seconds, a child springs forth, another life is born. My baby's passage down the birth canal was pure excitement, a very spiritual experience. I had thoughts about the miracle of life—how incredible it is creating another person together. To see it happen right there before your eyes, you feel the power of a spiritual force greater than the two of you."

Suzanne Arms

Another new father sees it as *magic:* "When the baby finally came out, it was a magical experience. My partner and I looked at each other and looked at our child. Our tears were just falling. I couldn't believe she was really there—such an indescribable feeling."

A third father is captured by its purity: "Looking at him, I'm dealing with a very pure experience that I can't really put into words. Seeing him emerge, I thought, 'My son.' I could hardly comprehend what was going on. I knew he was my son. This realization was almost overwhelming. *Here's my son.* I wanted to holler or cry or do something . . . anything."

A fourth father calls it *amazing:* "It was just phenomenal how our baby was born. It is enough to make you wonder. This was the most amazing experience I've ever had. Nothing will ever be like this."

A father of premature twins was overcome with *reverence.* Setting his newborns next to each other, he lowered his face to theirs and told them, "Alexandra, Gabriella, I'm your daddy. I love you with all my heart. I'll always be here for you," then gently placing one hand on each tiny head, proceeded to recite a Hebrew blessing for them.

Along with each of these feelings come *self-transcendence* and *deep communion*. As Damian puts it: "I cried, feeling a strong sense that we had created something together. We had endured a crisis. Later, I looked at Sally resting on Toni's stomach. I was having my experience with Sally—feeling full of joy and astonishment—then I felt Toni's feelings too. We were feeling together . . . just so close."

Trevor speaks of "immersion." He explains: "I do not know what I was *thinking* during the experience. I do remember being fully attentive to Karen and what was happening to her, fully trusting in her and following her instructions."[24]

Gazing at his newborn, a father feels *proud* as well. "The whole experience of seeing your baby and smiling and having everybody around you saying 'congratulations' and patting you on the back is incredible," says one man. "You're immediately recognized in the role of a father. . . . That was a very significant thing for me." A child often represents a great personal accomplishment, a feat that enables the father to say to himself: "I've done it. I'm really a man now. I've endured one of the hardest experiences in my life, and I can do it again." In this sense, the child gives birth to the father.

Suzanne Arms

A new father may take special satisfaction in seeing his likeness in his child. Noting a physical resemblance confirms his paternity and may set him on an unexpected road to personal renewal. Alan describes his experience in these terms: "When I look at my son and see things about him that resemble me, or a picture of me as an infant, I think, 'What a remarkable experience—to live that part of myself that I never ever saw, or did see and can't recall.'"

Filled with this potent sense of fatherhood, a man begins a new chapter in his life. He develops ties with his forebears and, in the process, catches glimpses of his own immortality.

Laboring and Birthing Apart

Witnessing labor and childbirth places a man next to his partner and illuminates his commitment to the relationship and to his paternity. The intense drama that ensues can awaken within him unanticipated responses, exposing his strengths and vulnerabilities, hopes and fears.

Don, not quite ready to step into his new role, describes this frightening aspect of his experience: "I was really shocked by the birth. I was prepared for a beautiful, fantastic experience. I watched, however, with disbelief as the baby popped forth all of a sudden. After a while, it hit me—this was my baby, half me and half my wife. I looked at my wife and for a moment forgot the baby was there. It was automatic. . . . It had always been just the two of us. Now we're three."

Don is not alone. Many fathers attending childbirth have trouble relating to the event. Some are struck with fear. Others get caught in the grip of early negative conditioning about parenthood. Still others—consciously or unconsciously defending against the reopening of old wounds related to childhood neglect, rejection, or abandonment—approach childbirth with ambivalence or distaste, or avoid linking themselves to the event altogether.

If you are willing but not ready to participate fully in labor and birth, take heart. Although old emotional patterns are often deeply and painfully embedded, they can be uprooted. Psychological defenses do soften; emotional wounds heal. And fatherhood can provide the remedial "tug."

Begin by realizing that you are *not* responsible for the fears, conflict, and confusion you may be feeling at this turning point in your life. Rather than view these responses as character flaws, see them as manifestations of your childhood conditioning. Avoid blaming yourself for being ambivalent or aloof, and instead direct compassion to the parts of you that were not nurtured in childhood.

Recognize, too, that athough you are not responsible for what happened to you in the past, you *are* responsible for creating a healthy and loving life for yourself and your new family. This means deciding to break free of the negativity of past; to heal old wounds; to cast off your self-blame, guilt, and self-denial; and to be the person you want to be *now*. Participating in childbirth is one way to disengage from painful encumbrances and start fresh. *Missing it, however, is no major calamity.* Fatherhood offers endless opportunities for self-renewal.

Jim did not participate in his son Joey's birth and for some time afterward worried about their future together. A year later, he wrote to tell me: "Joey calls me 'Dada' now and jumps for joy when he sees me come home from work. I can hardly believe it. The other night, I swept him up in my arms and hugged him for a long time. He smiled a big smile. I started to get teary. I can't remember my father ever being there with me this way. I never really knew why. I thought there was something wrong with me or he would have liked to play with me. There were a lot of things in the past—emotions locked up, unexpressed. . . . I cried some more later that night. It was like I had taken off the lid a little and was finding feelings I never knew I had. I was finding myself, releasing myself, balancing the scales."

Welcoming Your Baby

Perhaps the most impressionable moments in a child's life are the minutes and hours after birth. Imagine being enfolded in warmth, darkness, and the steady pulsations of a heartbeat for nine months, then suddenly emerging into the world as we know it. No wonder the newborn begins the business of bonding immediately upon being touched, fed, and talked to.

Jack Heinowitz

The importance of early, uninterrupted bonding has received so much recognition in recent years that increasing numbers of parents who give birth in hospitals are requesting one-on-one time with their newly born babies. Hospital administrators, convinced that immediate parent contact is of great benefit to babies, have begun altering policies to increase the amount of time newborns can spend with their parents.

Bonding has a less publicized aspect too: the attachment process works *both* ways. As a newborn unites with mother and father, so do mother and father unite with their newborn. For a father, particularly one who was not present at the birth, immediate contact can evoke a deep sense of connection, pride, and accomplishment. The more opportunities he has to focus all his attention on his newly born child, the more involved he is likely to become with his child. Author-researcher Martin Greenberg, MD, calls this type of fatherly contact "engrossment," and considers it an innate potential shared by all men. His research suggests that a man who is initially reluctant to engage as a father can push through his detachment simply by becoming engrossed with his baby.[25]

A man who becomes engrossed with his newborn is profoundly rewarded. As Larry says, recalling his first hour of fatherhood: "I really loved it when he just looked at me. Once in a while, I saw an intense stare. I got such a big kick out of that. We're talking about a very special moment—a relationship—my son looking at me and me looking at him, feeling like we're equally fascinated. That was an extremely powerful experience."

Make every attempt to initiate this experience with your child directly after birth. If immediate physical contact becomes impossible due to a medical emergency, request to be as close to your newborn as possible. Russ's son was born by cesarean and whisked off to the nursery while his father nervously paced the floor of the father's waiting room. Watching his baby intently through the observation glass immediately afterward afforded Russ a desperately needed release and a critical first opportunity for bonding. He describes the experience this way: "In the waiting room I felt trapped. I just kind of endured the chatter and my worries about Leslie and the baby. I had no place to go. Then, seeing Sammy there in the nursery, all I wanted to do was stand still and watch him. It was an overwhelming feeling of fascination, like he was the first baby I'd ever seen. I just didn't want to move from that spot."

Participating in a cesarean is of course far more advantageous—for father, mother, and newborn. On the scene, you will be able to stroke and cuddle your baby right away. Aware of the tactile and emotional needs of the moment, you can request that your baby be brought to mother's bedside so that she, too, may extend her touch of love.

Whether or not your child is born by cesarean, take advantage of rooming-in policies and extended visiting hours for fathers and siblings. This is a prime time for family bonding. As one new father comments, "The fact that I was able to see my daughter and see the difference in her growth during the first three days of her life really helped me know her."

Homebirths, although free of medical and scheduling restrictions, pose challenges of their own. Homebirthers are often faced with an endless stream of visiting friends and a constantly ringing telephone. If you are planning a homebirth, remember to tape up the doorbell and post a Family Bonding notice on the front door, leaving a pad and pen outside for well-wishers. Also record a birthday greeting on the answering machine, and turn off the phone. Friends, neighbors, and relatives will be glad to have their calls returned *at your convenience.*

Whether your child's birth takes place in a hospital, a birthing center, or the master bedroom, take all the time you need to welcome your baby into your family and into your heart. Also do whatever you can to preserve the sanctity of the mother-child bond. Keep mother and baby warm, free of intrusions, and well nourished. Arrange for healthy meals, change diapers, and stay close to the nest. In short, follow your fatherly instincts.

Suzanne Arms

When the cry of the newborn enters your lodge, consider it singing, and it will not be so annoying.

—Shaman Chief Kitpou

CHAPTER 10

STEPPING INTO PARENTHOOD TOGETHER

My expectations were that once we had the baby, this was to be the climax and everything would be sort of uphill from there—all would be glorious and beautiful. Well, it has been good for the most part, and yet there are some very firm adjustments that have to be made.

SETTLING BACK INTO LIFE WITH AN INFANT is anything but "settling." Everything has changed. Expectancy has fast-forwarded into moment-to-moment unpredictability. Morning routines are no longer limited to the morning, are no longer routine, and sometimes do not occur at all. The addition of a tiny new family member heralds an entirely altered reality.

As most new parents begin replacing familiar routines with the responsibilities of caring for their child in the postpartum days, they realize how unprepared they are for parenthood. They also discover that, contrary to popular opinion, parenting is not all instinctual; indeed, a great deal of effective parenting hinges on *trial and error.* Like any new process riddled with unknowns, this one takes time to adapt to.

Time Out for Adjustments

If you are feeling frustrated and disillusioned, join the crowd of parents who every day are discovering that no amount of prenatal preparation can prepare us for the ever-changing demands of new parenthood. In the career of parenting, there is no substitute for *hands-on experience.*

Interestingly enough, in acquiring this experience, you will retread many of the emotional trails you have recently traveled. Your enthusiasm may again wane; irritation may intrude. If so, steer clear of self-criticism. Colliding emotions are as endemic to the postpartum weeks as they are to pregnancy. Embrace the contradictions, and forge ahead

Who Am I Now? Who Are You? Childbirth transforms wives into mothers, husbands into fathers, lovers and partners into parents, and small families into seemingly enormous ones. Although you may expect to carry on much the same as always, you are not likely to ever wake up feeling as you did before, for you are a changed man.

John, a first-time father, was startled to find this out at the start. "Going through the birth with my wife was a milestone, a definite change," he relates. "I can't really explain how, but I know it had a profound impact on me, to the very core of my being—a change in my inner self. There was just no way for me to really predict how it would be, how *I* would be. All the preparation I did helped me think about being a good father; it didn't prepare me, though, for the impact that being a father would have on my life."

Scott's discovery was more circuitous, for he launched into the postpartum period focused squarely on his partner. Although he appreciated her attachment to their son Chris, he was agonizingly aware that "she was no longer girlfriend or lover." This sense of loss led him to thoughts of his childhood. Memories of his mother's early warmth and availability filled him with new feelings of respect and admiration for his wife's nurturing qualities. Recalling his father's "distance and businesslike demeanor," Scott became cognizant of his unsatisfied needs for closeness with his father. In touch with his "father hunger," he felt saddened and began grieving for the father love he had never known. Soon afterward, his orientation shifted: thoughts of missing his partner-as-lover turned to desire for contact with his newborn. Now, three weeks past this turning point and feeling recognized by his son, Scott is ecstatic. "To see him react to me, just lighting up like a Christmas tree," he says, "has to be one of the greatest, most exhilarating feelings a man can have. And that happens almost every night when I get home. Things are sure looking up now."

At some point soon after childbirth, more surprises will come to light. Life without your newborn, for example, may suddenly seem like a distant memory. As a first-time father comments after only one week of parenthood, "I can hardly remember not having a child at home." Just as suddenly, amid the excitement and joy of snuggling in with your baby, you may feel sad about the irreversibility of being a parent. And naturally so, for in greeting the present, we say farewell to the past.

Three for Tea. The early days of parenthood often trigger strikingly different reactions in mothers and fathers. Following childbirth, a new mother may mourn the loss of a special period in her life. Gone is the ineffable relationship with her unborn child. Gone, too, is the attention bestowed on her as a pregnant woman. What's more, hormonal shifts, physical healing, and anxiety about meeting a spectrum of expectations—her child's, her husband's, her extended family's, and her own—can leave her feeling bewildered, guilty, blue, or just plain exhausted.

Christine describes her early postpartum experience in these words: "I'm responsible for this new life . . . the baby depends on me. I'm supposed to know instinctively what a mother does to care for an infant, but I don't. I never spent much time with babies. . . . I'm afraid that my husband sees my inadequacy with the baby—that I'm letting him down. He does his job well, providing for me and the baby; I feel like I'm *failing* at mine. I think he's angry with me because things aren't going more smoothly around the house. I haven't been making his lunch or taking care of him as usual, but I'm tense and tired and afraid to show him I need him. Everyone has advice for me—Grandmother, the neighbors, other relatives. Why do they all have so much advice? They must think I'm doing a bad job."

Your partner desperately needs your thoughtfulness and consideration at this time. To support her efforts, try stepping outside yourself. Refuse to take her lack of energy as a personal insult or rejection. Rather than lament the lack of attention coming your way, appreciate her struggle. Your sensitivity to her needs can greatly ease her transition to motherhood.

Men enter parenthood with somewhat different vulnerabilities.

The birth of your child, for example, may have set off an unparalleled emotional high, a surge of pride and self-esteem. Now that you are "settling in" to the reality of caring for your newborn, you may be apprehensive. If so, have patience—self-assurance will come as you get to know your baby. Many men have difficulty relating to a brand new baby. Some require substantial amounts of time and interaction before comfort and ease set in. Others prefer to step back and observe more experienced caretakers, or look to their partners for the guidance and validation needed to gain confidence in themselves.

Regardless of where you stand on the comfort continuum, you can begin forming a *strong relationship* with your baby early on. Spin a cocoon around hearth and home after birth, honoring the importance of privacy, quiet, and help from neighbors and friends. Acknowledge that your partner's hormonal system is not the only one radically altered at this time—yours is too. Endorphins are still pumping. You may be living in a dream state, sleepwalking the trails from bedroom to kitchen, bathroom to bedroom. Nature, it seems, has fashioned this state of timelessness to help parents recover their ener-

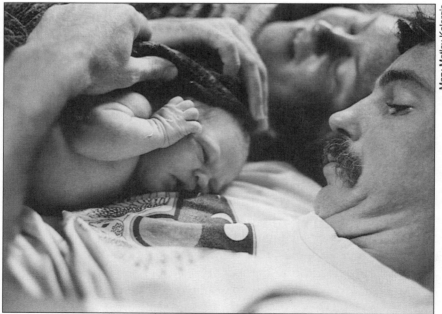

Mary Motley Kalergis

gy after childbirth. Relax into the dreamtime. Relish in it. Think about adopting baby's sleep-wake pattern for a while. Being in sync at the start will automatically nourish your father-newborn connection.

Remember, though, that this delicate bubble of timelessness can be pierced; the sweet ambience, easily disturbed. The more you leave the house, the more you will be wrenched out of the postpartum time zone and hurled into one governed by jarring external circumstances. And once this bubble has popped, it is gone forever. The secret to family bonding—the balm for both of you—is to stay quiet, remain close by, and take your time stepping out of the stillness. Consider the period after childbirth a honeymoon. Some postpartum couples "honeymoon" for a month before going out in public.

While on retreat, every new mother and father must be nourished, and this is where friends and relatives come in. When friends and family members want to know what they can do to help, tell them, "Dinner!" Let them deliver meals to your doorstep, everything from beverages to desserts, forks to dishes. Friends and loved ones will enjoy creating sumptuous offerings to celebrate the new family and, when requested, will be happy to respect your need for sanctuary.

I Can't Get No Satisfaction. As the weeks go by, you may look to your child for a smile, a touch, a sign of interest in you as Dad. Until you see your first glimmer of recognition, take pleasure in knowing that your child is drawing comfort from your touch, a sense of belonging from your gaze, and contentment in the warmth of your arms. Be patient; keep up the holding, touching, and stroking; and prepare for that spontaneous moment in which your child will *overtly* delight in your presence and seek out your attention.

Tom, four months into fatherhood and close enough to look back clearly on this interlude in his life, reflects: "I was disappointed that more didn't happen in the beginning. I remember putting my finger in my son's hand, just wanting more physical contact. I was hoping he would react to me in some way . . . but no. He was fitful and maybe not too happy about being jerked into the world. I would have liked to have held him, to have been with him more in his first few days of life."

Jerry, equally frustrated by his son Jarrod's apparent unresponsiveness, disengaged and waited for a sign of recognition from him.

By the time Jarrod was three months old, Jerry, still "unrecognized," was feeling terribly unimportant. To make matters worse, he began comparing his father-child relationship with his wife's mother-child relationship. "Jarrod is an active baby, yet I can't get a whole lot of feeling from him," he mentioned one day. "My wife, of course, felt communication almost immediately. She felt a give-and-take there all along. But I couldn't. There is a limit to what I can do with Jarrod. It is really frustrating!"

Warren also experienced a delayed reaction in attaching emotionally to his infant. For several months after Jill's birth, Warren was "anxious," "scattered," and disappointed in himself for feeling "so removed" from his child. "It's as if in my mind there's a nonreality about having a child," he told me. "I'm living these experiences, but every once in a while, I catch myself realizing that I've been in a state of shock. I'm kind of detached from the whole thing."

Speaking with other parents, increasing his participation in household chores and child care, airing his feelings with his wife, and spending time alone with Jill lifted Warren out of his fog. Now, a month later, he remarks: "It's so beautiful having her here. She's opened up my feelings of love. Just holding her and looking at her, living with her. It's amazing, but I almost enjoy changing her diapers and cleaning up after her. I don't even feel resentful. Maybe I was a mother in a past life, or something." Maybe he was actually a *fatherman*.

The more opportunities you take to rock, walk, sway, talk to, sing and dance with, or simply watch your infant, the more confident you will become and the more inclined you will be to work cooperatively with your partner. Spend plenty of time together clarifying frustrations, exploring preferences, and enjoying each other's company. Open communication is a stellar tonic for the isolation and insecurity that often plagues fathers *and* mothers in the earliest stage of parenting.

So Who Comes First? The onslaught of adjustments and compromises demanded of new parents can be staggering. Suddenly, in addition to maintaining a home and livelihood, you must tend to a constant round of feeding, bathing, changing, and comforting. (Yes, infants *do* require constant surveillance.) If you have older children, they, too, will be looking to you for help—not only in meeting their customary needs but in adjusting to the new arrival. With very short notice, you have been called upon to suspend your own needs and interests and cater to your newborn's, your older children's, and each other's. No wonder the first year of parenthood is considered the most sensitive and stressful period in a couple's relationship!

Naturally, adjustments of this magnitude do not come without complaints. The most common gripes of new mothers include lack of sleep, time, and energy; feeling confined; feeling socially isolated; loss of spontaneity; loss of income; guilt about not being a better mother or partner; decline in housekeeping standards; disappointment with the father's level of involvement; and disenchantment with parenthood.

Here is one mother's wish list: "I wish someone would help with the added work around here. I wish my husband would get up at night once in a while to help with the baby. I wish I weren't so exhausted all the time. I wish I could just ask for the help I need instead of pushing myself so hard to avoid neglecting anyone else's needs. I wish I didn't think I had to be perfect to deserve some help or attention or TLC."

New fathers report similar misgivings. Men gripe about their partners' diminished attention, availability, and sexual responsiveness as well. Some also feel excluded from the relationship their partner is forming with their child; others, concerned that they may "never" adjust to fatherhood, worry about the possibility of another pregnancy in the near future.

Alex, expecting that his relationship with Carla would "spring back to how it was before Lori was born" grew increasingly disillusioned. Carla was extremely tired in the first postpartum months and seemed "irritable" and "demanding." When their baby was three months old, Alex shared his frustration with me, explaining: "My wife's energy isn't back up yet. Our energy levels are so different now. She's pooped at six o'clock, and I'm raring to go. Every once in a while, my angry feelings come out. I say something that puts extra demands on her. I feel like I shouldn't, but I do anyway."

Alex tried to adjust by embarking on numerous projects at home. He remained frustrated, however, resenting the intrusions posed by Lori and Carla's demands. In time, he became critical of Carla. Because she was reluctant to leave their daughter with friends or relatives despite his coaxing, he accused her of being insecure about motherhood. He also chided her for not spending enough time out of the house. Only in subtle ways did he begin admitting to his own insecurity and need for time alone with Carla. As he mentioned to me one afternoon: "Carla and I used to share almost everything we did, and now we can't because it's hard for her to get away from the house. So I stay home with Carla and Lori. It feels pretty OK to go out and do something myself, but I want to be out with Carla."

Reprioritizing is easier said than done. While respecting your partner's fatigue and your baby's needs, you may have conflicting needs of your own. If socializing with friends is important to you in the early postpartum months, consider doing it on your own. If what you want is time alone with your partner, let her know, preferably with "I" statements. Gradually try reconciling your desires with your newborn's need for a harmonious parenting alliance, hours in-arms with mother, and involvement with *you*.

Feeling Left Out? Simply understanding a newborn's continual need for mother's milk and attention does not keep a man from feeling jealous of his partner's deep involvement with their child. Jealousy and envy are natural responses in the early weeks of fatherhood. Fleeting spells of these emotions need not cause difficulties; experienced repeatedly over long durations of time, however, they can become highly problematic, particularly when the father feels routinely excluded from the mother-infant dyad.

Some new mothers *do* keep the father at a distance. This dynamic is often prompted by the mother's insecurity (needing the child nearby), possessiveness (wanting the child for herself), or anger and resentment (keeping the child to herself to punish her partner).

By the same token, a new mother sensing her partner's lack of responsiveness to her or their newborn will feel excluded from *his* world. In the words of one distraught woman: "I don't understand why my husband seems so disinterested in the baby. He's too busy . . . other things are more important. He said before we were married that he really wanted children, but he doesn't seem to

---

LETTING IN THE ODD MAN OUT

A new mother harboring frustration or resentment toward her partner might explore the following questions:

- Am I having trouble letting my partner close to me or our child? If so, why?

- Is my partner's closeness threatening to me? If so, how?

- Do I feel hurt by him? If so, how?

- Am I treating my partner the way I saw my mother treat my father?

---

want this one. Each time he ignores the baby, I take it as a rejection of me. I thought of the baby as a gift to him, an expression of my love. He's telling me it's not enough—not good enough. *I'm* not good enough."

To effectively keep a new mother's feelings of exclusion at bay, the father can offer generous amounts of emotional support ("I'm here to listen and help") and validation for her mothering ("You're doing a great job") while monitoring any resentment he may be feeling toward mother or child. Resentment, hard to recognize, may be disguised as guilt, overgiving, stoicism, displaced anger, irritability, or withdrawal, or concealed beneath physical complaints.

In short, both of you may feel left out during the emotionally delicate newborn period. If signs of emotional withdrawal appear, take heed. Tapping in to the source of the problem can quickly widen the family circle.

Is There Sex after Birth?

The postpartum period is a sexually sensitive time for most couples. To begin with, women are often conflicted about resuming

ADJUSTING TO PARENTHOOD

To run a status check on your feelings about parenthood and your relationship, answer these questions:

- Have my feelings toward my partner changed? If so, how? Why?

- Has my partner changed? If so, how? Why?

- Does my partner treat me differently now? If so, how?

- Do our childrearing values jibe? Do we have a harmonious approach to discipline? Are we in accord about fulfilling our newborn's needs, giving attention and reinforcement, divvying up the childcare tasks?

- Do we get our frustrations off our chests? If so, how? Do we argue over the real issues, or do we get sidetracked? Do we feel better or worse after venting our conflicts?

- Since becoming a parent, have I changed my priorities? If so, how?

- Am I satisfied with our social life, our sex life, our relationship?

intercourse in the weeks following childbirth. To compound the issue, health-care providers frequently prescribe a waiting period of four to eight weeks—advice that accommodates some women and frustrates others.

Following childbirth, a woman begins stepping fully into motherhood, adjusting to breastfeeding and infant care, recovering from physical discomfort and fatigue, and waiting for her body to acclimate to its nonpregnant condition. For a month or two, her interest in lovemaking may be at an all-time low. Still in the throes of plummeting estrogen levels and completely "touched out" by the end of each day, she may not want more body stimulation. Conversely, as soon as her uterine discharge has cleared, she may feel ready and eager to resume lovemaking but, perhaps confused by her care provider's instructions, unsure about whether or not to proceed. A call to her practitioner may help resolve the dilemma. Most importantly, she must feel *at ease* with her decision to resume or delay intercourse.

Her partner is sure to have predilections of his own. A man eager to resume lovemaking may find a wait of any duration too long and drawn out. As one new father puts it, "It's as though we really haven't been with each other lately, even though we seem to be together more." Some men express their disappointment by pouting and withdrawing; others actively complain and make excessive demands. In response, and to avoid angering their partners, some women return to lovemaking before they are ready—a mistake best nipped in the bud. When "giving in" becomes habitual, anxiety mounts and resentment sets in.

Then, too, a man may have a diminished interest in lovemaking, due either to the dramatic adjustments required in caring for his newborn or to feelings of jealousy and exclusion from the mother-infant "couple." A fretful baby, broken sleep, or frequent nightwaking will exhaust any parent. Jealousy can stem from sexual frustration or the father's perception that his partner's erotic needs are being satisfied by the baby. Fathers of breastfed babies, in particular, are relieved to learn that what is arousing the mother is not the baby, but the *mother's own body.*

Despite any prenatal promises you have made to not let your baby interfere with your relationship, baby's needs, as you have no doubt discovered, do come first. Spontaneity must be suspended for a while. But keep the faith—it will return. In the meantime, plan romantic interludes around your infant's schedule, and take full advantage of nap times. The sacrifice in spontaneity is a small price to pay for a flourishing baby and a loving partnership.

Breastfeeding can pose additional challenges to sexual intimacy. For one thing, the mother who nurses on demand is in a constant state of readiness: her infant cries, and her milk lets down. Some women say that the sensation of leaking milk interferes with love-making; others find it enjoyable. For another, when the baby cries during lovemaking, a nursing mother must choose between her own gratification, her partner's, and her infant's. Meanwhile, her partner must decide whether to assert his desires or defer to his child's needs. Some amount of frustration and conflict is obviously unavoidable. To prevent the buildup of antagonisms, think *patience* and *creativity*. Well-minted humor can be a godsend.

Then, too, while breastfeeding, a woman may experience sensations akin to orgasm. These sensations originate in uterine contractions induced by the infant's suckling. Depending on how the woman perceives her experience of arousal, it may stimulate or diminish her desire for sexual contact with her partner. Furthermore, a breastfeeding woman is likely to experience increased breast tenderness, sore nipples, and decreased vaginal lubrication—all of which can detract from pleasure during foreplay and intercourse. Physiological changes of this sort are typical of the early postpartum period, and *couples who anticipate them have little difficulty easing their way back to full-spectrum sexuality.*

The father of a breastfed child undergoes alterations of his own. Watching his child nurse, he may entertain a variety of thoughts, feelings, fantasies, and associations. Seeing his partner as mother rather than lover may consciously or unconsciously thwart his longing to reestablish a sexually intimate relationship with her. Conversely, the image of his child at peace at the breast may inspire boundless love and reverence for his partner. He may derive deep contentment while snuggling close to the breastfeeding pair. Fascinated and excited by his partner's nursing breasts, he may want to taste her milk during their love play. Cultural taboos aside, the fulfillment of this desire is a source of pleasure and intimacy for many couples.

Perhaps the most common concern facing fathers of breastfed babies is fear of being shut out of the feeding relationship. Jim expresses it this way: "I'm able to participate in baby care and take part in a number experiences with our baby, but I can offer no assistance at night when my wife is nursing the baby. I've got no choice. There is no reason even to get up. . . . I feel bad. I wish I

Suzanne Arms

could help out, but I can't do anything. If I'm not a part of it all, then something's missing. It shouldn't be my wife's responsibility to raise a child. It should be an equal kind of arrangement." There may indeed be "no reason to get up," although a diaper change, night walk, or baby burping is bound to be welcome.

If you are feeling banished from the feeding relationship, try not to take offense. Instead, nestle with the nursing pair, resting your hand gently on baby's back. At nonnursing times, bring baby to *your* breast. Cuddling, walking, and relaxing with your infant supported against your bare chest will provide your infant with warmth and invigorating skin-to-skin contact—two nutrients babies need in vast quantities. Shower with baby tucked in close to your chest. (Do not worry about smothering your newborn; by nature's design, babies' nostrils flare out to the sides to facilitate breathing in close quarters.)

All the while, support the nursing relationship. Your ongoing encouragement can help desensitize your partner to negative associations she may have with her breasts. In fact, women who, as a result of sexual abuse in childhood, have entered motherhood with an aversion to breastfeeding, often heal their trauma by nursing their babies.

In short, a father has many ways of nourishing his breastfed infant. Chief among them is the *pleasure he generates* in knowing his child is receiving the best substance nature has to offer. Nothing supersedes mother's milk as a source of balanced nutrition, a wellspring of natural immunity, and a major stimulator of brain development. The father who creates a safe, homey setting for his new family can rest assured in knowing that he is a father-man in the truest sense of the word.

The immediate postpartum period, although filled with challenges, is no time to stop making love. Your partner needs to know that she is still attractive and desired. And you need to know that you are still number one. So check up on your relationship. If your sex life is suffering, make intimacy your first priority. Meeting each other's needs for closeness, affection, and sexual stimulation is the surest way to hasten your transition to passionate lovemaking.

For now, go gently and tenderly. Intercourse during this period may be most comfortable in a side-by-side or female-superior position, which will afford your partner some control over the depth of penetration. She may especially enjoy slipping off to a quiet, private place with you to make love after breastfeeding. Pleasure and satisfaction can also be found through mutual massage, bathing, sharing fantasies, and other forms of noncoital sexual activity. Talk about your changing sexual feelings with each other. Remember that physical discomforts will soon pass and that the lovemaking you embark upon then can be better than ever.

Jan Francisco

We don't just care for our children; we're taking care of them. We're not only working to provide for our families; we're working to be present with them.

—Emery Bernhard

CHAPTER *11*

CLEARING THE HURDLES OF INFANCY

If anyone had told me this is what parenting an infant would be like—actually, a lot of people did back then—well, I wouldn't have believed it. The fascination, the love I feel, and all I'm learning about kids is marvelous . . . but when do those days of a solid sleep, clean home, and time alone return? Pretty soon now, I hope.

AS THE POSTPARTUM INCUBATION PERIOD gives way to day-to-day realities, life becomes eminently practical. Uncertainty evaporates like a mist: baby is either visibly content or not, and mom and dad are unequivocally wanted and needed. Much of the inner dialogue fades, for there is a great deal to tend to in the outer world.

The key to meeting the exigencies of infancy is to fuse the inner world that has become known with the outer one that is rapidly introducing itself. The result: an underlying harmony that can last throughout year one and on into the future.

The Stresses of New Parenthood

With a new being in your midst, *everything* is new. Time evaporates every so often. Your relationship to friends, relatives, career, and certainly your partner is now superimposed on a larger reality— your connection with your little one. Once-minor inconveniences may seem like major pushes and pulls. In every aspect of your life, the sanest, surest road to travel is the path of least resistance.

Fatigue. Exhaustion triggers irritability, impulsivity, and sometimes poor judgment—not the most desirable qualities to bring to

153

parenthood. To avoid fatigue and sleep deprivation, cut out all unnecessary activities. For restful nights, bring baby into bed with you, reserving lovemaking for other times and places. Research amply demonstrates that family sleeping is not only safe but conducive to family bonding and well-being: parents sleep better and babies, exposed to the stimulation of a regulated heartbeat, are helped to overcome possible tendencies toward sleep apnea.[26] To slow your pace in the daytime hours, wear your baby. Carried in-arms—or in a sling, a soft frontpack, and later, a backpack—your infant will be soothed by the warmth and gentle motion of your body, and will be able to view life from a vantage point very close to your own.

Visitors. You may be tempted to encourage visits from friends and relatives. It is natural to want to share your joy and sense of accomplishment, show off your baby, or solicit a helping hand. Realize, however, that although friendly visitors may be supportive at this tender time, they can also intrude on your privacy and interfere with your adjustment to parenting and partnering.

Visitors—even loved ones—may add stress to your life. Visits from parents, especially, can hurl you back emotionally into the role of child. You may suddenly be responding to your parents' expectations, attitudes, and values about childrearing instead of your own. Weigh these considerations carefully, and discuss them with your partner before opening your door to company.

Siblings. Young siblings conceptualize the arrival of a new baby much as they do the arrivals they are familiar with, such as a new toy that can be discarded when interest dwindles or a visitor who leaves after a short stay. Not even older siblings, better able to grasp the implications of having a new baby in the house, can imagine the impact it will have on established family dynamics. When the baby at last arrives, siblings of all ages share a common fear: that they will be replaced by the intruder or abandoned by Mom and Dad.

Regardless of how well you have prepared your child for the new arrival, count on witnessing some or all of the following responses: *ambivalence, resentment, jealousy,* and *regressive* (baby-like) *behavior.* Also expect fluctuations in your child's adaptation to the baby. Whatever responses you observe, consider them expres-

Leah Olman

sions of the adjustment your child is undergoing. If your baby's needs have been consuming vast quantities of your time and attention, you may very well be "turning away" from your older child. Outbursts of anger or ongoing jealousy can be a wake-up call from a child whose fears of abandonment have not yet been put to rest. Regressive behavior may indicate that your child is reexperiencing the past to prepare for "stepping up" now that a *real* baby has joined the family. If your child begins acting like an infant, realize that developmental forces are at work. Allow for the temporary comfort available in trying out the little one's sleeping quarters or in making baby sounds. Acknowledge the struggle ("It's hard having a baby around"). Your understanding and acceptance can ease the transition for your child and promote a sense of accomplishment all around.

Here are some additional guidelines for facilitating sibling adjustment and bonding:

- Share basic information about infant development: size, weight, and sensory and physical capabilities. Answer all questions frankly and simply. Following your child's lead will prevent you from giving more information than he or she wants or is capable of comprehending.

- Allow for the expression of all feelings. Rather than intruding with judgments and censorship, help your child identify the emotions that are surfacing. (For assistance, refer to the listening and communications skills discussed in chapter 8 and the illustration on pages 28–29.) Share *your* feelings as well. Explain that this has been a difficult time filled with changes, that you are irritable (impatient, grumpy) due to lack of sleep, that your moodiness is not your child's fault, and that the emotional climate will soon improve. Ask if there is something special your child would like from you. Or ask your child to make five wishes and share them with you. These activities can clue you in to the needs that require your attention.

- Set aside time each day to be with your child. A bedtime bath, story, or review of the day, along with good cuddling and loving words, can help offset insecurities. Take your child to work with you, or launch into a special project together at home. *Let your child in on your world.*

Suzanne Arms

- If you are going out, allay anxiety by telling your child where you are going and how you can be reached.

- Welcome your child into the new triad with group hugs and family playtime. Welcome all requests to participate in baby care, showing your child how to hold, play with, diaper, and bathe the baby. Supervising each step of the way, acknowledge your child's patience, helpfulness, and gentleness.

- Shepherd your child into a community of valued friends, trusted neighbors, caring coworkers, and other acquaintances. A sense of community can provide much needed security, a feeling of inclusion, and an enlarged context for the exchange of affection and exposure to role models. Extending the family in this way will provide your child with places to go in times of feeling misunderstood, alone, or trapped.

Work Arrangements. Do what you can to avoid diving back into the work force full-time. The drain on your energy as well as the fragmentation you will feel upon leaving home for the workplace may not be worth the financial gains of a forty-hour-a-week commitment.

To ensure that you and your family are well cared for, take a generous parental leave. When it draws to a close, consider slowing down your career, postponing or refusing promotions, cutting back or eliminating travel, or establishing a work arrangement that will allow for plenty of family time. Explore creative options such as flextime, a compressed workweek, annual hours (scheduling time off for now and arranging to meet the required number of annual hours by year's end), part-time work, job sharing, and flexplace (working offsite at your home). Some new fathers elect to join the 41 million-and-growing homeworker force. Others spend the first year of their child's life on leave, a sabbatical, or a career break. At-home dads form a rapidly growing sector of today's population.

If you are unable to restructure your work life for the first nine to eighteen months of fatherhood, create a schedule that will allow you to return home for lunch or midafternoon breaks. Even then,

you may feel tugs of remorse or anxiety about leaving your partner and baby. If so, do not fight them; call a truce and surrender. Do not be embarrassed about missing your baby either. Your fathering coworkers may already have a sneaking suspicion that babies need their dads close by, and vice versa. Call often during the workday to see how your infant is doing and how your partner is faring.

Parenting Arrangements. When it comes to household chores and child care, what *specifically* do you expect of yourself and your partner? Is your current allocation of responsibilities suitable, or are modifications needed? Are you feeling pressured to work toward an equal division of parenting responsibilities? If so, does this arrangement suit you and your partner, your work situations, and your relationship? If not, find a balance that works better for both of you. What counts is your *unity of vision,* not some predefined parenting arrangement.

If you have not already done so, draw up an agreement for domestic responsibilities. Build in rewards for meeting the stated terms—a favorite dessert, an afternoon hike, or perhaps hot-tubbing by candlelight. Reevaluate your agreement as the need arises.

The "Perfect Parent" Trap. A teacher of mine once professed, "Anything worth doing is worth doing poorly," probably never imagining how suitable the adage is to parenting. Adopt it for a while, and see how things go. Permit yourself and your partner to make mistakes—lots of them. They'll happen anyway, and you will benefit enormously from them. Be *who you are,* imperfections and all. Let your child see you fumble. What better way is there for a youngster to learn that mistakes are essential to growing up and growing wise?

Talk to your partner and friends about your previous experiences with children, your own childhood, and what you did and did not learn about parenting. Appreciate how unfamiliar you really are with parenting and the enormity of the task before you. Beware the perfect parent trap, and strive to be simply a *good* parent.

While you are at it, remember that being a good parent means being a good partner. Do not allow your child's needs to obscure your desire for time with your partner. Be honest and direct with each other. Avoid placing your child's needs between you. Say, "I

HERE AND NOW

To evaluate your present situation, fill in the blanks below:

- The hardest topic to discuss with my partner is _____ because _____.
- The most difficult aspect of being a parent now is _____.
- The worst aspect of being a parent now is _____.
- The best aspect of being a parent now is _____.
- What I'm learning from being a parent is _____.
- What I've lost by being a parent is _____.
- What I want most now from my partner is _____.
- What I want most now from my children is _____.
- What I want most now from my friends is _____.
- What I want most now from my relatives is _____.
- My greatest asset as a parent now is _____.
- My greatest asset as a partner now is _____.
- What I need to work on most is _____, and I'm going to start by _____.

really *don't want to* go out now (or make love now)" rather than "I *have to* take care of the baby now." And do not criticize your partner's parenting. Be sensitive to each other's concerns and competence levels.

A Father's Touch

Child care is a father's issue. It is in "tending to" that deep fibers of connection are woven between father and child. Many aspects of child care, however, may at first seem awkward, unpleasant, frightening, or simply unfamiliar. With experience, you will master them—and much more besides.

Crying. Babies cry to let us know they are uncomfortable, in pain, hungry, wet, needing to burp, sick, too hot, too cold, overstimulated by their environment, or missing their caretakers. Breastfed babies cry when they are sensitive to a substance the mother has ingested; common culprits include cow's milk, iron-fortified vitamins, excessive amounts of caffeine, and certain medications. Formula-fed babies cry in response to substances they have ingested; typical offenders include soy, highly acidic juices, some formula components, and certain teas.

Many fussy babies are soothed by holding, massage, motion, fresh air, music, singing, and invariably, suckling. Although what "works" one day may not do the trick the next, some approaches to infant crying are predictably reliable. Researchers have found, for example, that infants who are held the most, even while asleep, spend the least amount of time crying. Studies also show that a parent's response to tears and fussiness has everything to do with the development of trust in infancy. *Being there at crisis time* lets your baby know that the world is a safe, caring place and that you can be counted on as a source of security, support, and love.

How do you respond to your infant's tears? If after you offer measures of comfort your infant is *still* upset, do you feel sad? If so, invite the sadness in—it is a healthy, wholesome response to your child's pain. Do you instead feel angry? If so, acknowledge your anger and examine it. Several studies reveal that parents who cannot tolerate the sound of a baby crying were frequently not picked

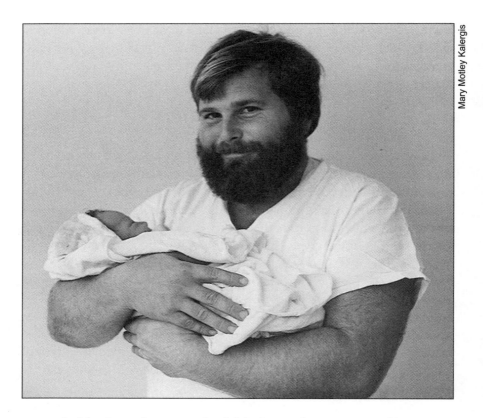

Mary Motley Kalergis

up or held when *they* were fretful babies. The practice of leaving a baby to "cry it out"—touched off most often by parental frustration—may be another conditioned response stemming from a history of unanswered calls for help.

If you find your baby's crying objectionable or discomforting, mentally note your reaction, then *go to your child*. Massage away the tension that has accumulated. Hold your baby—rock, sway, sing your favorite song. If the crying continues, seize the opportunity to release some tears of your own. Crying is especially therapeutic after a difficult or birth, recollections of unhappy childhood memories, or simply a frustrating, stressful day.

Diapering. Routines established in infancy form long-lasting sensory impressions. So it is of great value to diaper with special mindfulness, with kind, tender, even playful attention focused entirely on your baby. The emotions you bring to diaper changing will help mold your baby's body concept. If feces or urine are disgusting to you, your infant will sense your displeasure and may have difficulty developing a healthy body image or personal hygiene habits in the years ahead.

Rather than scrunching up your nose and commenting on the "yukkiness" of it all, try to regard each diaper change as a love offering. Then offer your diapering love *frequently*. Many families in cultures that view diapering as a sacrament change their babies' diapers twenty or more times a day.

Bathing. Water is more than a cleansing agent; it helps mediate emotions. Hence, bathing your baby may be the perfect end to a busy day. The safest and most comfortable ways to bathe a baby are while standing at full height (propping baby up in a soft container in the sink or on a foam pad or towel placed in the sink), sitting in the tub with baby held close, or cradling baby against you in the shower.

Whether you decide on the kitchen sink or the bathroom tub or shower, be sure the site is draft free. The water, a tad cooler than what you may be accustomed to, should feel warm to the inside of your wrist. Use a secure fatherly hold while lowering baby into the sink or entering the water together. With a soft washcloth, gently wash your baby all over. The attitude conveyed in your strokes and facial expressions will be the message your infant takes in, so dispel any fears you may have about being repulsed or aroused by your baby's body. Have the emotion, then bathe your baby.

Independence? The frontier spirit continues to guide many parenting philosophies. We sometimes think that babies must be "taught" independence and "socialized" as early as possible. In truth, expectations of this sort run counter to everything we know about infant development. Genuine independence grows naturally out of a childhood in which *dependency needs have been met*. Socializing, in the usual sense of the word, is beyond the capacity of infants.

What babies need most is consistency of care, touch, loving responsiveness, and *time to be babies*. Human infants, unlike most animal neonates, have a long period of dependence. Researchers point out that humans require six to nine months to achieve levels of physiological maturation attained by other primates shortly after birth.[27] To accommodate the physiological immaturity of human babies, some perinatal specialists recommend following up the nine months of intrauterine gestation with nine months of extrauterine gestation.

If your goal is to father a healthy, autonomous child equipped to develop strong relationships with others, avoid the temptation to encourage early weaning in the interest of "getting" your infant on "real food." Similarly, reject all well-meant suggestions to hire a string of round-the-clock baby-sitters to "accustom" your infant to a "variety of caregivers." The way to independence and socialization is through a long and fulfilling stage of dependence—on Mom and Dad.

Nurturing the Nurturers. While caring for your baby through the first year of life, take special care of yourself and your partnership. Keep your feelings and needs out in the open. When disagreements arise, remind yourself that the culprits are not your feelings and needs, but rather your *denying* and *withholding*.

Remember, as the months go by, that you and your partner are journeying together. You are both trying to juggle your child's changing needs with your own. Look to each other, and ask each other for help. Check out the assumptions you are harboring. Every so often, conduct a reality check: "I think you feel (want) _____. Is that true?" Schedule fun and intimate times together. Rekindle the past. Get reacquainted.

Growing a Nontraditional Family

The days of the Traditional Family are over. Today's families come in all shapes, sizes, and configurations. As established as this fact may be, people living in once-stigmatized family constellations still encounter considerable discrimination. Cultivating a healthy, wholesome nontraditional family in today's world is a complicated endeavor; nevertheless, it is achievable, and with mastery comes an extraordinary sense of fulfillment.

Perhaps the most important first step is to recognize that a nontraditional family will never become a traditional family. It can, however, become a fulfilling form of kinship for all family members.

Marilyn Nolt

Teen Parenting. Teenage fathers are the most overlooked and least understood group of parents in today's culture. If you are among them, you may have to work hard to retain your rights and privileges as a father, and even harder to dispel the crippling myths associated with adolescent fathers—the majority of whom are decidedly *not* promiscuous and *not* reluctant to provide their families with emotional and financial support.[28]

As a new father, you may want to reach out for vocational, financial, or legal counseling; early parenting education; or psychological counseling to help you combat the stresses of early parenthood. You and your partner will need all the support you can mobilize to stay in school while earning an income and fulfilling your parenting and partnership responsibilities. As intimidating as this balancing act may seem for now, realize that the future looks promising. Recent findings show that when a teenage father sustains his partnership and actively participates in parenting, his child develops fewer behavioral problems, higher self-esteem, and higher levels of social competence than one whose adolescent father has remained absent from the home. Furthermore, the majority of young men who complete programs in parenting skills and infant development become responsible and caring parents.[29] Teenage fathers need *support* and *guidance,* not stereotyping and downgrading.

Fathering through Divorce. The divorce rate in the United States has tripled over the past thirty years. Today, men between the ages of twenty and forty-nine currently spend an average of only seven years living with their young children.[30] No longer can we pretend that the birth of a child will cement a shaky relationship. Indeed, a partnership that lacks a strong foundation is at great risk of crumbling under the stresses and strains of early parenthood.

Following my own divorce and joint custody settlement, I worked long hours with divorced fathers wanting more involvement with their children. Sadly, the majority of these men had, upon separation, left their homes and children, and subsequently failed to assert their desire for or right to regular contact with them. Some tried, but stopped short when faced with resistance. Most, out of frustration, powerlessness, or insecurity about their importance to their children, remained only passively involved, remote, and largely unavailable. Many were playing out unfinished business with their ex-partners. Many more were unconsciously reenacting dramas associated with the fathering they received.

These divorced fathers were seeking information, support, and encouragement for taking the legal and emotional steps needed to reunite with their children. Each man spoke of a persistent emptiness—a void dug deep by both his own father loss and his longing to be close to his children. Each man also mentioned that while working hard to provide for family well-being, he had unwittingly sacrificed the intimacy and connectedness that had animated his earliest days of fatherhood. As time passed, these men had grown tentative and uncertain about their ability to play with their infants. Leaving became easier. Staying away followed naturally.

Something, however, was now pulling these fathers out of their anger and discouragement and back to their children. Perhaps it was their acknowledgment of that dark hole. Or maybe it was the close, personal bonds established with their little ones during and after childbirth. Whatever their individual calls to action may have been, they illustrate a collective reality: *men who experience the unparalleled joys and rewards of fathering are not likely to relinquish their relationships with their children upon dissolution of their marriages.*

If you are in the midst of a separation or divorce, hold fast to your child. Despite the bitterness you may be feeling, let your father love flow. Remember that the person you are disengaging from is your spouse, not your child. If you are thinking of relocating to another city or state, do reconsider; your infant will need ongoing tangible reminders of your affection. If your infant is breastfeeding, arrange for a parenting schedule that will allow for continued nursing and frequent portions of daddy love. Rise above your animosity and, setting all sights on your child, negotiate a mutually agreeable parenting plan with your former partner. For help in mediating a postseparation arrangement based on your child's emotional needs, contact your county court, a family mediator, or a family therapist.

Families of Mixed Heritage. Parents with different racial, ethnic, cultural, and religious backgrounds have the challenging task of cultivating self-esteem, pride, self-acceptance, and family identity in children who are apt to encounter minority prejudice and disdain. Sad but true, our culture still regards children of mixed heritage with discomfort, if not out-and-out contempt.

Francis Wardle—an English-born author, educator, and father married to a woman of African American, Native American, and Asian descent—offers parents the following encouragement:

- Take pride in your ethnic, racial, and historical background. Treat all religious, national, cultural, and linguistic differences in your family with respect and understanding.
- Celebrate the courage of your decision to parent together. Approach childrearing as an affirmation of your love and belief in equality, and with full awareness that differences and uniqueness are gifts to be treasured. Decide together on ways to help your child take pride in these qualities and learn to deal with insensitive remarks.
- Address the question of identity early on—before others in your child's world do it for you. As time goes on, answer all your child's questions openly, accurately, and simply. Explain that physical characteristics come from *both* parents. Point out that physical variations also arise in the natural world of plants and animals.
- As the years pass, talk regularly about your encounters with curious, ambiguous, or judgmental reactions to multiethnic realities. Invite your child to do the same.
- Fill your home with food, artwork, music, and literature that reflect cultural diversity. Exposure to biographies of men and women of mixed heritage will enhance your child's sense of belonging.
- Advocate for your child. Do not let professionals try to convince you that mixed heritage is the cause of any problem or that your child should be raised solely in the minority culture.[31]

Epilogue

WHEN LOVEMAKING LEADS TO CONCEPTION, more than one seed is planted. As new life takes form, we undergo an unfolding of our own. We move from seeing ourselves as children of parents to finding a new identity as parents of children. Gradually and surely, a startling realization dawns: *we are being re-created by our creation.*

The transition to parenthood is an extraordinary, exciting, frightening, confusing life passage filled with unfamiliar, changing, and often contradictory emotions. Everything is tested—our flexibility and endurance, our adaptibility and capacity for interdependence, and our commitment to personal and partnership growth. Around each bend in the road are rich opportunities for reevaluating the past and setting new goals, discovering and developing new aspects of ourselves, and appreciating ever new facets of our partnership. With the birth comes prodigious growth. Parenthood itself challenges us to risk, stretch, and transcend our own needs; to cultivate patience, trust, forgiveness, and humility; to learn nurturing and empathy; and to love unconditionally.

There is magnificent order and purpose in this journey you have undertaken. There is consolation, too, in knowing you are on a two-person adventure. Set forth together, trail markers in hand. Living your journey every day, you will deepen your relationship with yourself, each other, your child-to-be, and *all* that is still to be born.

APPENDIX A

CARING FOR THE PREGNANT COUPLE

PROFESSIONAL CAREGIVERS PERFORM A SPECIAL SERVICE in the life of a child-bearing couple. As a childbirth educator, labor assistant, or health-care provider, you are certain to be one of the few people privy to the deeply personal concerns of the expectant mother and father. For the father, in particular, you may be the sole source of emotional support. As such, your openness and encouragement are vital.

Equally essential is your capacity to incorporate the psychological and interpersonal aspects of pregnancy into your standard of care. To truly assist the pregnant couple, we as perinatal professionals must move far beyond physiological technicalities in our discussions and presentations; we must become sensitized to the *many* aspects that contribute to well-being in the childbearing months. We must, in short, become experts in the art of communication and the science of the heart.

Self-Help Tips

To promote an emotionally healthy pregnancy for your clients, begin with a self-check. What are your most firmly held values and priorities? What are your strengths and difficulties in working with expectant couples? How familiar are you with the growing body of literature on the psychology of childbearing? If you need to brush up on your knowledge of pregnancy-related feelings, fantasies, and needs, by all means do so. A wealth of information is now available (see pages 181–184).

Also clarify your attitudes about being pregnant and being a parent. Do you have unfinished business with your parents, partner, or birth practitioner? If so, how does it influence your interactions with clients? What subtle messages might you be conveying? What types of situations or questions arouse your confidence, anger, anxiety, resentment? Examine the unspoken content of your discussions and presentations, and flush out unwanted biases and predisposing beliefs that may negatively impact on your clients' experience of pregnancy.

Finally, boost your understanding of interpersonal dynamics, and polish your communication skills. Begin by looking closely at your personal and professional relationships. Do you consistently provide reliable feedback and information? Are you generous with your attention? Are you able to let go of old entrenched behavior patterns? Can you risk being wrong? Do you ask for what you want and need? Is your receptivity in good working order?

Remember that what you are sharing with your clients is more than facts and data—it is a *way of being*. Knowledgeable and savvy in relationship dynamics, you will be equipped to model the behavior of an open, nonjudgmental listener—precisely what you would want your clients to aspire to.

Expanding Your Repertoire

To assist your clients in approaching pregnancy and childbirth with confidence, you will want to foster an awareness of feelings and attitudes, a climate of honest sharing, and the expectant father's inclusion in the childbearing process. Toward that end, try integrating some of the following ideas into your office visits or class curriculum:

- Discuss the value of pregnancy rituals for both partners. If you are a class teacher, compile a list of your students' rituals to pass out in class.

- Alert couples to the wide range of feelings that arise in pregnancy and to the importance of identifying them (see chapters 2 and 8). If you are working with a group, take a poll of the emotions already evident.

- Advise expectant parents to alternate between "he" and

"she" when referring to their unborn child. The purpose is twofold: to inspire discussion of set preferences and to help couples adjust to the possibility of having a child of either gender.

- Ask partners to compose letters to each other, their unborn child, and their parents. Sending the letters is less important than expressing the sentiments.

- Help couples adapt to the realities of parenting. If you are a teacher, invite new mothers and fathers to return to class, infants in tow, to share their experiences.

- Encourage couples to form a pregnancy task force—a network of professionals who can be counted on to answer questions as they arise. If you offer classes, solicit participation from midwives, doulas, obstetricians, pediatricians, nurses, anesthesiologists, mental health professionals, childbirth educators, and lactation consultants.

- Address prenatal and postpartum sexuality as well as the benefits of breastfeeding and its impact on the partnership.

- Provide opportunities for expectant fathers to meet on their own to address fathering feelings, preferably with a male facilitator. If you conduct classes, separate the men from the women and ask both groups to talk about their relationship concerns; then bring the groups together to check out each other's assumptions.

- Introduce the notion of role reversal. Ask couples to switch roles and, playing each other, discuss a topic such as What I'm Liking Most about Pregnancy, What I'm Needing Most Right Now, Some of My Concerns, or any relevant theme. This exercise is best performed in pairs or small groups, and is most helpful when followed up with conversation about the issues that are raised. During the conversation, partners can take turns letting each other know if they feel understood and if their feelings and experiences were captured accurately. For a variation on this theme, ask couples to switch roles for labor practice. Reversing the laborer-labor partner arrangement gives an expectant mother and father a chance to view the situation from each other's perspective. Moreover, reversing the giver-receiver pattern furnishes the man with nurturance and attention, restoring balance to the give-and-take pattern of the relationship.

• Emphasize the importance of mutual touch and massage. Expectant fathers are often advised to massage their partners during labor—an effective activity that many mothers recall not only during birth but afterward. The expectant father, however, needs soothing as well. If you are a childbirth educator, consider allotting a segment of class time to mutual massage, an activity that can address the needs of *both* parents and help offset imbalances in the relationship. One creative teacher asks each woman to role-play her uterus while her partner takes the part of the fetus. As a tape of fetal sounds plays in the background, the women slowly curl themselves around their partners. Then husbands and wives switch roles.

Ellen Eichler

SUPPORT ORGANIZATIONS

Academy of Certified Birth Educators
11011 King, Suite 111
Overland Park, KS 66210
800-444-8223

Alternative Childbirth Educators
PO Box 1286
Placentia, CA 92670
818-445-5126

American Academy of Husband-Coached Childbirth
PO Box 5224
Sherman Oaks, CA 91413
800-42-BIRTH

American College of Nurse-Midwives
1522 K Street NW, Suite 1000
Washington, DC 20005-1299
202-289-0171

ASPO/Lamaze
2931 South Sepulveda Boulevard, Suite F
Los Angeles, CA 90064
310-479-8669

Association for Childbirth at Home International
PO Box 39498
Los Angeles, CA 90039
213-667-0839

Association for Pre- & Perinatal Psychology & Health
1600 Prince Street, Suite 500
Alexandria, VA 22314-2838
703-548-2802

Austin Men's Center
700 West Avenue
Austin, TX 78701
512-477-9595

Birthworks
42 Tallowood Drive
Medford, NJ 08055
609-953-9380

C/ SEC, Inc.
22 Forest Road
Framingham, MA 01701
508-877-8266

Doulas of North America
1100 23rd Avenue East
Seattle, WA 98112

Family & Work Institute
330 Seventh Avenue
New York, NY 10001

The Fatherhood Project
Families and Work Institute
330 Seventh Avenue, 14th Floor
New York, NY 10001
212-465-2044

International Cesarean Awareness Network
PO Box 152
Syracuse, NY 13210
800-695-4276

International Childbirth Education Association
PO Box 20048
Minneapolis, MN 55420
800-624-4934

La Leche League International
PO Box 4079
Schaumburg, IL 60168-4079
708-519-7730

Midwives' Alliance of North America
PO Box 175
Newton, KS 67114
316-283-4543

NAPSAC
Route 1, Box 646
Marble Hill, MO 63764
314-328-2010

National Association of Childbearing Centers
3123 Gottschall Road
Perkiomenville, PA 18074
215-234-8068

National Fatherhood Initiative
600 Eden Road, Building E
Lancaster, PA 17601
800-790-DADS

National Men's Resource Center
PO Box 800
San Anselmo, CA 94979
415-453-2389

New Ways to Work
149 Ninth Street
San Francisco, CA 94103

Postpartum Support International
9271 Kellogg Avenue
Santa Barbara, CA 93117
805-967-7636

Teen Father Collaboration
Bank Street College of Education
610 West 112th Street
New York, NY 10025

Work/Family Directions
930 Commonwealth Avenue
Boston, MA 02215
617-278-4000

1. *The Most Important Thing You Can Do for Your Children Is to . . . Be Their Dad* (Lancaster, PA: National Fatherhood Initiative, 1994).

2. S. Keen, *Fire in the Belly: On Being a Man* (New York: Bantam, 1991), pp. 47–48.

3. C. Zolotow, *William's Doll* (New York: Harper Collins, 1972), pp. 30, 32.

4. R. Louv, *FatherLove* (New York: Simon & Schuster, 1993), p. 31.

5. C. Stevens, "Father and Son," *Tea for the Tillerman* (Ashtar Music, 1970).

6. H. Chapin, "Cat's in the Cradle," *Harry Chapin: Anthology of Harry Chapin* (Elektra/Asylum Records, 1985).

7. J. B. Franklin and C. M. Franklin. *Fatherbirth: The Challenge of Becoming a Male Parent* (Self-published, 1987), p. 11.

8. H. B. Biller, *Fathers and Families: Internal Factors in Child Development* (Westport, CT: Auburn House, 1993), ch. 2.

9. Ibid.

10. Ibid.

11. J. Collins, "My Father," *Who Knows Where the Time Goes* (Rocky Mountain National Park Music, 1968).

12. See also J. L. Shapiro, *The Measure of a Man* (New York: Delacorte Press, 1993), ch. 1.

13. A. Colman and L. Colman, *Pregnancy: The Psychological Experience* (New York: The Seabury Press, 1973), pp. 103–104.

14. W. H. Trehowan, "The Couvade Syndrome," in *Modern Perspectives in Psycho-Obstetrics,* J. G. Howells, ed. (New York: Brunner/Mazel, 1972), pp. 83–86.

15. Ibid. pp. 68–93.

16. See Notes 13, 14, and 15.

17. N. Hall and W. R. Dawson, *Broodmales: A Psychological Essay on Men*

in Childbirth (Dallas, TX: Spring, 1989).

18. P. Brenner, *Life Is a Shared Creation* (Marina del Rey, CA: DeVorss, 1981), p. 159.

19. See Note 2, p. 227.

20. *The Tribal Laws of the Children of Light,* S. C. Kitpou, comp. and trans. (unpublished), p. 3.

21. E. Bing and L. Colman, *Making Love during Pregnancy* (New York: Bantam, 1977), p. 28.

22. Ibid.

23. A. Montagu, *Touching: The Human Significance of the Skin* (New York: Harper & Row, 1972), p. 96.

24. T. Herriot, "Husbandry amid Wives," *Mothering* 73 (Winter 1994): 74–79.

25. M. Greenberg and N. Morris, "Engrossment: Newborn's Impact on the Father," *American Journal of Orthopsychiatry* 44 (1974).

26. The effects of family sleeping on the breathing patterns of infants and its impact on Sudden Infant Death Syndrome (SIDS) has been extensively researched by J. J. McKenna. See J. J. McKenna, "An Anthropological Perspective on the Sudden Infant Death Syndrome (SIDS): The Role of Parental Breathing Cues and Speech Breathing Adaptations," *Medical Anthropology* 10 (1986): 8–92; J. J. McKenna, S. Mosko, C. Dungy, and J. McAninch, "Sleep and Arousal Patterns of Co-Sleeping Human Mother/Infant Pairs: A Preliminary Physiological Study with Implications for the Study of Sudden Infant Death Syndrome (SIDS)," *American Journal of Physical Anthropology* 83 (1990): 331–347; and J. J. McKenna, "SIDS Research," *Mothering* 62 (Winter 1993): 45–51.

27. H. E. Fisher, *Anatomy of Love: The Natural History of Monogamy, Adultery, and Divorce* (New York: W. W. Norton and Company, 1992), p. 231.

28. B. Robinson, *Teenage Fathers* (Lexington, MA: Lexington Books, 1990), ch. 2.

29. R. Stengel, "The Missing Father Myth," *Time* 90 (9 Dec 1985): 49.

30. Taylor, "Two Faces of Fatherhood," p. A–1, cited in R. Louv, *FatherLove* (New York: Simon & Schuster, 1993), p. 98.

31. F. Wardle, "Raising Interracial Children," *Mothering* 58 (Winter 1991): 110–117.

REFERENCES AND SUGGESTED READING

Anderson, Sandra VanDam, and Penny Simkin. *Birth—Through Children's Eyes*. Seattle, WA: Pennypress, 1981.

Arms, Suzanne. *Immaculate Deception II: Birth & Beyond*. Berkeley, CA: Celestial Arts, 1993.

Arms, Suzanne. *Seasons of Change: Growing through Pregnancy and Birth*. Durango, CO: Kaviki, 1993.

Balaskas, Janet. *Active Birth*. Boston: Harvard Common Press, 1992.

Baldwin, Rahima. *Special Delivery*. Berkeley, CA: Celestial Arts, 1990.

Biller, Henry B. *Fathers and Families: Internal Factors in Child Development*. Westport, CT: Auburn House, 1993.

Bing, Elisabeth, and Libby Colman. *Making Love during Pregnancy*. New York: Bantam Books, 1977.

Bowlby, John. *Attachment*. New York: Basic Books, 1992.

Bradley, Robert A. *Husband-Coached Childbirth*. New York: Harper & Row, 1965.

Brenner, Paul. *Life Is a Shared Creation*. Marina del Rey, CA: DeVorss, 1981.

Bridges, William. *Transitions: Making Sense of Life's Changes*. Reading, MA: Addison-Wesley, 1980.

Carter, Lanie. *Congratulations! You're Going to Be a Grandmother*. New York: Pocket Books, 1980.

Chamberlain, David. *Babies Remember Birth: And Other Extraordinary Scientific Discoveries about the Mind and Personality of Your Newborn*. New York: Ballantine, 1990.

Colman, Arthur, and Libby Colman. *The Father: Mythology and*

Changing Roles. Wilmette, IL: Chiron Publications, 1988.

Colman, Arthur, and Libby Colman. *Pregnancy: The Psychological Experience.* New York: The Seabury Press, 1973.

Franklin, John B., and Cherie Martin Franklin. *Fatherbirth: The Challenge of Becoming a Male Parent.* (Self-published) 1987.

Greenberg, Martin. *Birth of a Father.* New York: Continuum, 1985.

Griswold, Robert L. *Fatherhood in America: A History.* New York: Basic Books, 1993.

Harper, Barbara. *Gentle Birth Choices: A Guide to Making Informed Decisions.* Rochester, VT: Inner Traditions, 1994.

Hotchner, Tracy. *Pregnancy and Childbirth: The Complete Guide for a New Life.* New York: Avon, 1984.

Keen, Sam. *Fire in the Belly: On Being a Man.* New York: Bantam, 1991.

Kitzinger, Sheila. *Giving Birth: The Parents' Emotions in Childbirth.* New York: Taplinger, 1971.

Kitzinger, Sheila. *Your Baby, Your Way: Making Pregnancy Decisions and Birth Plans.* New York: Pantheon, 1987.

Klaus, Marshall, and John Kennell. *Bonding: The Beginnings of Parent-Infant Attachment.* New York: NAL, 1983.

Liedloff, Jean. *The Continuum Concept: Allowing Human Nature to Work Successfully.* Reading, MA: Addison-Wesley, 1985.

Lindsay, Jeanne Warren. *Teen Dads: Rights, Responsibilities & Joys.* Buena Park, CA: Morning Glory Press, 1993.

Louv, Richard. *FatherLove: What We Need, What We Seek, What We Must Create.* New York: Simon & Schuster, 1993.

Marnie, Eve. *Love Start: Pre-Birth Bonding.* Santa Monica, CA: Hay House, 1989.

Marshall, Connie. *The Expectant Father: Helping the Father-to-Be Understand and Become a Part of the Pregnancy Experience.* Citrus Heights, CA: Conmar, 1992.

Montagu, Ashley. *Touching: The Human Significance of the Skin.* New York: Harper & Row, 1972.

Mothering Magazine, eds. *Being a Father: Family, Work, and Self.* Santa Fe, NM: John Muir Publications, 1993.

Nilsson, Lennart. *A Child Is Born.* New York: Delacorte Press, 1990.

Osherson, Samuel. *Finding Our Fathers: How a Man's Life Is Shaped by His Relationship with His Father.* New York: Fawcett Columbine, 1986.

Peterson, Gayle. *Birthing Normally.* Berkeley, CA: Mindbody Press, 1984.

Peterson, Gayle, and Lewis Mehl. *Pregnancy As Healing: A Holistic Philosophy for Prenatal Care.* Berkeley, CA: Mindbody Press, 1974.

Rapoport, Rhona and Robert N., and Ziona Strelitz. *Fathers, Mothers, and Society: Perspectives on Parenting.* New York: Vintage Books, 1980.

Schwartz, Leni. *Bonding before Birth.* Boston: Sigo Press, 1991.

Sears, William. *Becoming a Father: How to Nurture and Enjoy Your Family.* Franklin Park, IL: La Leche League International, 1986.

Sears, William. *Nighttime Parenting: How to Get Your Baby and Child to Sleep.* Franklin Park, IL: La Leche League International, 1985.

Thevenin, Tine. *The Family Bed: An Age-Old Concept in Childrearing.* Wayne, NJ: Avery, 1987.

Verny, Thomas, and Pamela Weintraub. *Nurturing the Unborn Child: A Nine-Month Program for Soothing, Stimulating, and Communicating with Your Baby.* New York: Delacorte, 1991.

Verny, Thomas, with John Kelly. *The Secret Life of the Unborn Child.* New York: Dell, 1986.

If you would like to order more copies of

Pregnant Fathers: Entering Parenthood Together

by Jack Heinowitz, PhD, please call

1-800-356-9315

(ordering service: Upper Access)

Also available from Parents As Partners Press:

Poster—"A World of Feelings" by Betsy James, as seen in chapter 2 of this book. A handy learning device measuring 17 by 11 inches, for adults and children **$7.95***

Bumper sticker—"I'm a Pregnant Father," distinctively decorated with a father stork **$3.95***

Pamphlet—"Being Pregnant Together: The Changes Involved in Becoming Parents." To receive your copy, please send a self-addressed, stamped business envelope to the address listed below . . . . **Free**

Please photocopy this page or print your order on plain paper, indicating the quantity you want of each item, and send with your name, address, and a check or money order to:

Parents As Partners Press
4019 Goldfinch Street, Suite 170-B
San Diego, CA 92103

* Postage paid (California residents, please add 7.25% sales tax).